Needs ABC
Acquisition and Behavior
A model for group work and other psy...

New Groupwork Book Series edited by Tim Kelly

Needs ABC
*Acquisition and Behaviour Change
A model for group work and other
psychotherapies*

Tom Caplan

W&B

MMVIII

© Tom Caplin 2008
Published by Whiting & Birch Ltd,
Forest Hill, London SE23 3HZ

EAN 9781861770530
ISBN 1861770537
Printed in England and the United States by Lightning Source

Contents

Acknowledgements ix

About the author x

Introduction 1

1. **Group therapy:**
   Definition, indications and contraindications 5
   Who benefits from group therapy? 7
   What makes a group? 7
   What makes someone a group therapist? 8
   How does group therapy succeed? 8
   When therapy in a group is not appropriate 9
   Why the Needs ABC? 10
      Cognitive-behavioural therapy 10
      Motivational therapy 10
      Narrative therapy 11
      Emotion-focused therapy 11
   The Needs ABC's defining goals 12

2. **A good therapist** 13
   The possession of relevant qualifications 13
   Awareness of the utility of life experience 14
   Facilitation skills 14
   Awareness 15
   Objectivity 15
   Respect 16
   Gender awareness 17
   An understanding of cultural issues 18
   Self-awareness 18
   Ability to stay on track 19
   Onward and upward 19

3. **Creating a productive therapeutic setting** 21
   Practical issues in group work 22
   Components 22
   First impressions: From the telephone to the screening interview 23

The screening interview. 25
Preparation for a Screening Interview. 28
Screening as therapy. 30
When individual therapy is necessary before group meetings 32
Getting the ball rolling: First group encounters 33
Helping a group to form the Needs ABC way .34
Maintaining a group. 35

4. The Needs ABC Model in practice 37
Group process/client process 40
The incoming client stages: The McGill Model. 41
   1. The 'safety' stage. 41
   2. The 'social' stage 43
   3. The 'inclusion' stage 45
   4. The 'collaboration' stage 46
   5. The 'continuity' stage 48
The usefulness of co-facilitation and therapist teams 49
Closed vs. open groups. 51
Group and client process in action. 52
Challenging, linking and inclusion techniques 55
   Supportive challenging. 55
   Mentoring 57
   Linking and inclusion 58
   Group linking. 58
   Client-paced work 59

5. Introducing the 'universal themes' 61
Family of origin/latency. 64
Cultural difference/human sameness 68
Different themes can lie behind similar behaviours. 71
   Common behaviours. 71
   Common treatment expectation versus diverse
   perceptions of treatment goals 72
   Standardised and individualised therapist treatment goals 72
Addressing unmet needs in group context. 73
   Emerging theme. 73
   Avoiding being driven by a curriculum 74
Tools that can help 75
   Feelings chart 75
   Role play 75
   Time-out, logging and business meetings 76
Recognising the emotional component of the universal theme 77

A model for group work and other psychotherapies

6. The uncovered needs-deficit and what to do with it 79
   Isolating universal themes 80
      Abandonment 80
      Betrayal 80
      Intimacy 80
      Respect 81
      Competence 81
      Responsibility 81
      Power 81
      Grief/loss 82
   From the specific to the general 83
   Sustaining group process 94
   Needs vs. behaviour 94
   Universal themes and development 98

7. Eliminating barriers 101
   Creating a safe group work environment
      in which barriers can be breached 103
      Structure 103
      Facilitation 105
      Focus 106
   Importance of emotional safety 108
   Challenges to emotional group safety 111
   Challenges to emotional client safety 112
   Supportive challenges 113

8. How and when to intervene 117
   The power of the therapist 117
   Helping the group member to join 119
   Process theme versus content 121
   Timing 122
   Therapist self-disclosure 123
   Helping group members to take responsibility 124
      Maintaining the group's focus on its mandate 125
      Giving group members information about their behaviour 126
      Facilitating group discussion and dialogue 127
      Assessing the group member's emotional state 128
      Structured group exercises 130
   Helping the involuntary client 131

9. Family and couple work the Needs ABC way 137
   Applying the Needs ABC model to families and couples 140
   Combining group and couple work 147

Family therapy 150
Use of role play. 158
Therapist self-disclosure 160
Moving on. 163

10. After treatment. 165
Unplanned termination 167
Possible reactions to planned termination and
how to deal with them: Some examples. 168
Sadness 168
Anxiety. 169
Denial 169
Fear. 170
Relapse. 170
Flight 171
Tools to take to the world. 172

11. Student supervision 175
Teachers and students. 175
Being a student the Needs ABC way 176
Training as a group 178

12. Final comments 181

Notes. 189

Bibliography/references. 191

Figures

Fig. 1 Things are not always what they seem (gender-cultural) 17

Fig 2. Incoming client stages I: The 'safety' phase 42

Fig 3. Incoming client stages II: The 'social' phase. 43

Fig 4. Incoming client stages III: The 'inclusion' phase 45

Fig 5. Incoming client stages IV: The 'collaboration' phase. 47

Fig 6. Incoming client stages V: The 'continuity' phase. 48

Fig 7. Latency 65

Fig. 8. Feeling faces 87

Acknowledgements

The author gratefully acknowledges the help, support and caring of the following people:

Annette Werk for illuminating my competencies and guiding me towards their acquisition.

Deirdre Nuttall for her creativity, foresight and incredible skill.

Tim Kelly for his insight and helpful suggestions

David Whiting, my Publisher, for his patience.

A special note of thanks to Barbara Lang, my friend, partner and wife, for putting up with it all.

About the Author

Tom Caplan is a social worker in private practice who works with individuals, couples, families and groups. He is an adjunct professor at McGill University in the School of Social Work and Director and Supervisor of the McGill Domestic Violence Clinic. He is also a designated expert in Domestic Violence for the Quebec Court System. He undertakes clinical work with forensic populations, is the Clinical Director of the Montreal Psychotherapy Centre and is the founder and supervisor of the Montreal Anger Management Centre. Tom also presents workshops, gives trainings and lectures in universities, junior colleges and local community centres. He is engaged in ongoing research projects in collaboration with McGill University, Concordia University, the Jewish General Hospital and the Douglas Hospital. Tom is on the editorial board of *Social Work with Groups*, is a certified marriage and family therapist and a certified marriage and family therapy supervisor (AAMF.), an internationally certified alcohol and drug counsellor (ICADC) and a member of the Professional Order of Social Workers of Quebec (OPTSQ).

Introduction

THE MODEL PRESENTED in this book is applicable to group, individual, family and couple work and all of these therapeutic situations are addressed below, with a primary focus on its efficacy in group work.

Group therapy is, in a way, the Cinderella of psychotherapy, insofar as it is less widely available – despite its many virtues and capacities – than one-on-one therapy. It is certainly much less well understood, by members of the public who might benefit from it, and by many caring professionals themselves. There is a great deal of confusion surrounding the issue of what constitutes group therapy, and many resources that appear to offer group therapy, but do not. The ubiquity of self-help groups in the community – which can and do offer a useful service in their different ways – has led to public confusion about the difference between self-help and therapy.

As a therapeutic approach, group therapy has been around for more than five decades[2], but it seems that many helping professionals still do not have an adequate understanding of the internal dynamics of group work. In consequence, the extent to which they can provide adequate leadership to such a group can be seriously compromised.

Various excellent tomes on group work already exist. This one differs principally in the fact that its central message is about the commonality of emotional experience; how many people who – for widely diverging reasons – enter therapy, share emotions and problems based on those emotions that can be reduced to a relatively small number of core issues that are central to what makes us human, despite a multiplicity of maladaptive behaviours and personal circumstances. The same message can be applied equally well to other forms of therapy, including family and couple work, which are also discussed in this book.

The Needs ABC (Needs Acquisition and Behaviour Change) Model is dedicated to the exploration of these issues in a safe, client centred environment that allows group members to reach their own analyses of why they have sought help, and how they can start making things right. It is about wise leadership of the group but, much more than that, it is about facilitating individuals in their striving to take the reins of their own lives and emotions. Crucially, it is a model that is relevant to all individuals, regardless of gender, age, social class, ethnicity and level of education. Everyone's problems are unique, but emotions are universal and tend to be expressed in a limited range of ways, referred to throughout this book as the 'universal themes.'

Group therapy is an approach that can be of enormous help to the individual, to their families and those who care about them and, by extension, to our society. Couples and family therapy help to heal behaviours that will otherwise go on to create yet new generations of dysfunctional families. Helping people to deal with their problems in a constructive way as individual members of society has a profound, positive ripple effect throughout their communities, as removing dysfunctional responses to emotional pain leads to a very pragmatic reduction in domestic and other violence, alcoholism and substance abuse and the unhealthy family dynamics that can perpetuate problems through generations. Just to cite one example among an almost infinite number of contenders, it is widely recognised that physical abuse of children is frequently a learned behaviour passed from parent to child in a cyclical manner. Breaking this cycle can facilitate the creation of a healthier family dynamic and the cessation of such violence.[3]

The Needs ABC Model was originally developed by this author at the McGill Domestic Violence Clinic in Montreal, Canada. It uses an integrated therapeutic approach combining observation and elucidation of client and group process, using concepts also described in cognitive-behavioural, motivational, narrative and emotion-focused models.

What is that in plain English? Simply that the Needs ABC Model is about identifying clients' unmet relational needs; needs that can create a negative feeling which can, in turn, produce a maladaptive behaviour as a coping strategy. The unmet needs create emotions that may not be immediately understood and the emotion in turn leads to this maladaptive behaviour, which can manifest itself in an infinite variety of ways, but generally ways that are destructive to the individual in question, to all of those around them and, by extension, to society. Until these unmet needs are fulfilled, the maladaptive behaviour will continue. This is true in every case that brings an individual, group or family to therapy.

In putting the Needs ABC Model into practice, the counsellor's task is to identify the unmet needs that the client demonstrates – wittingly or unwittingly – when she[4] describes her life, her problems, and the reason or reasons why she has entered therapy. Once these needs have been identified, the counsellor's role must be to help the client to understand what these needs are and how they have arisen by using a process oriented, emotion-focused

A model for group work and other psychotherapies

universal theme paradigm. The counsellor must also assist the client in discovering alternative ways in which she can meet these needs; ways that are both functional and appropriate in the context of the society in which she lives. If the client acts to constructively change the way in which she is attempting to fulfil her unmet needs, her maladaptive behaviour, whatever it is, will gradually be extinguished.

This book will primarily focus on working within the context of a group, though the model itself can be used in all forms of treatment such as individual, couples and family work. Towards the end of this book, you will find a section on how to transfer the Needs ABC Model's interpretive skills to these modalities, as well as how group work training can be an asset in all of your therapeutic work, setting you apart from those who use the more traditional therapeutic approaches.

Understanding good group work practice will help you to understand how to give your clients the opportunity to discover how to acquire the power they need to make the changes they must to improve their quality of life; it will truly put the power to live in society in a healthful manner back into the hands of the people! Since all therapy is a form of social interaction and dialogue, understanding group work theory and practice should be a must for all clinicians who want to improve their ability to help others.

1
Group therapy

Definition, Indications and Contraindications

HOW CAN WE use apply group work strategies and techniques in a therapeutic context? You have undoubtedly heard the term 'group therapy' and feel you have a pretty good general idea of what is involved, but it is still worth clarifying what group therapy is and – equally importantly – what distinguishes it from other therapeutic approaches, as well as looking at when it is a good approach to take, and when it may not be.

Group therapy is a type of psychotherapy offered by a suitably qualified professional who works with several individuals (typically between five and ten) at the same time. The group leader's training and qualifications in the broader area of psychotherapy and specifically in group work are what distinguish group therapy from approaches such as self-help groups, in which people with similar problems may come together in an attempt to solve them, without the leadership of a qualified professional.

A number of people with problems they would like to solve coming together as a group does not of necessity imply that group therapy is occurring; for a group meeting to be group therapy takes trained leadership. This gives us our definition: Group therapy is a professional therapeutic approach headed by a suitably trained individual working therapeutically on problem-solving strategies with a number of people with similar problems at the same time, with the end-goal of achieving the remission of the undesirable behaviours or behaviour sets.

But why a group? What makes working in a group particularly apt for many people?

Because we are all members of society, and society is composed of many interlinking groups, group therapy is the extension into a therapeutic setting of the social way in which we live and of the social environment that has always characterised humanity. Life is all about how we interact with other people – family members, colleagues, friends, spouses, children – and most problems can be reduced at their most basic level to problems in the way in which these interactions take place. Group therapy is very different from the stereotype of one-on-one psychotherapy presented in so many Manhattan-based movies, and nor does it replicate the didactic approach of the 'twelve steps' approach. It is about learning and relearning how to be oneself in a healthy way in a social context. The social context, of course, consists of the norms and values commonly held by the majority in our society. A healthy relationship within society – with family members, friends, acquaintances and colleagues – does not, of course, mean pandering to the 'moral majority,' but it *does* mean understanding how one's chosen or given culture functions, and how its rules, limitations and possibilities can be negotiated in a productive way.

Group therapy can offer the ideal environment in which people with problems can come to terms with them, understand their causes and start working towards solutions and healthy coping mechanisms. The very fact of being a member of a group can be helpful, as it shows individuals that they are not unique in struggling at times, and provides all group members with the opportunity to learn from, and teach others. Group therapy has been around for many years[5], and has a great track record in helping people of all ages and both sexes come to terms with a wide range of problems, from substance abuse to bereavement, and everything in between. Group therapy provides a safe social environment 'outside' the realm of everyday life in which people can express themselves freely without fear of recrimination or punishment.

Individuals in therapy become not just people looking for solutions to their problems, but are also enabled to be people who can help others by offering insights and advice from their own experience.

In group therapy, problems that seem to overwhelm the individual are found to be issues that others face, too. In recognising others' dilemmas, problems in the way these are dealt with and possible approaches to take, group members can find the answers that they themselves are looking for.

It should be noted that, while group therapy has an 'end' in sight – the elimination of dysfunctional behaviours and their replacement with healthy behaviours – many people may benefit from attending more than one series of group meetings or even from attending group therapy throughout a relatively extended period. Some problematic behaviours, such as substance abuse, often require several episodes of therapy before the problematic behaviour is eliminated.6 However, the goal of group therapy should be not to transfer a dependence on a series of maladaptive behaviours to dependence on the therapist or the group, but to eliminating such dependence altogether; the end result of successful therapy is an individual who has learned how to interact healthily in her social arena and no longer requires therapy at all.

Who benefits from group therapy?

Group therapy can help people who struggle with their personal and professional relationships, who have problems with aggression, self-esteem or depression, who are trying to come to terms with loss or trauma, who are uncertain about or uncomfortable with their sexual identity, who have problems with substance abuse and self-destructive behaviours and a great deal more. While many people decide for themselves that it is time to start working towards solving interpersonal problems that have been making them feel unhappy or unfulfilled for years, others can be sent on an involuntary basis – often as the outcome of being tried in a court of law – to help them overcome problems with aggression, alcohol abuse, or other destructive behaviours. While the latter group represents some specific challenges to the therapist and the group, which will be discussed in detail later in this book, both voluntary and involuntary members can benefit greatly from group therapy.

What makes a group?

Depending on what the group needs to achieve and the individual requirements of group members, groups can include only members with similar issues or members with different sorts of issues. Similarly, the time frame of a group can be open ended or finite. The crucial aspect of the group should be its common focus, so that even when diverse problems have brought the various individuals to therapy, there must be a theme that brings them all together. For example, a parent who is violent towards children but not a spouse is unlikely to have the same issues as those addressed by men attending therapy for violence towards their wives. However, road rage perpetrators can benefit from therapy in the same group as those who are aggressive towards their colleagues. In the latter case, the common problem is 'violence' towards 'less intimate' people. Groups can be heterogeneous in terms of gender, race/nationality, income, etc. (with certain exceptions, which will be discussed later).

The dynamic that is formed by the various members of the group interacting, and going through a process of self and mutual discovery is what turns a 'bunch of people' into a group.

What makes someone a group therapist?

Generally speaking, a group therapist should have a strong background in psychology, counselling or a related field, and ample training in the specific area of group therapy. A group therapist must be able to lead a group and guide discussion without dominating. His or her role is to enable group members to speak for themselves and advise others, not to tell people how they should think and feel. Being an effective group therapist is a delicate balancing act that calls for empathy, emotional intelligence and academic knowledge! Group therapists should also have professional qualifications that are recognised by the relevant regulating body in the country, state or province in which they work. A group therapist needs to have an excellent understanding of psychotherapy, knowledge of the practical and emotional difficulties facing group members and the leadership and communication skills essential to heading a complex group of individuals. We will be discussing in some detail below what distinguishes a Needs ABC Model group leader.

How does group therapy succeed?

The chapters that follow will answer this question in detail. For now, however, suffice to say that a therapist selects a small number of people whose situations and personalities suggest that they will be able to work together, and assembles them as a group. The group meets on a regular basis to discuss, as openly and honestly as possible, the problems that have brought them to therapy and ways in which they can work together to help to resolve them. Many people need group therapy because they have problems of one kind or another with the way in which they relate to others. Being in a group in which communication is the very point of the exercise can help them to utilise latent communication skills and learn how to relate in a 'test' environment. Group therapy also offers the opportunity to use role play to 'act out' situations that are currently problematic, so that members of the group can experience and practice alternative ways of coping with stressors. To quote Kurland and Salmon, group work succeeds by giving its members the opportunity to 'gain from each other, to consider, to understand, to appreciate, and to build on each other's experiences, situations, problems, dilemmas, points of view, strengths and weaknesses.'[7]

When therapy in a group is not appropriate

Doing therapy in a group is applicable to a wide range of people and situations, but there are certainly times when it is not the right therapeutic approach to take, and knowing when to advise an individual to seek a different means of treatment is important. Group therapy can be enormously helpful to people suffering from problems relating to social anxiety, but it is not an appropriate treatment for people with severe psychosis or serious psychiatric illness such as schizophrenia that has not been adequately treated with the result that the condition is now in remission, although some forms of group work may be useful. Similarly, people who are feeling drawn towards suicide or murder or who are in serious crisis are not generally in a position to take part in group therapy until their situation has stabilised. People with serious intellectual limitations, such as severe Downs' syndrome or other brain dysfunction, may not be able to engage well with a group (although some intellectually disabled individuals can indeed benefit from group therapy).

Determining whether or not group therapy is appropriate to any given individual generally occurs during an initial evaluation of this person. A proper evaluation of any potential client prior to therapy is a must. At this time, it may be determined that some people are in fact good candidates for group therapy, but only following a period of one-on-one psychotherapy. Some of the categories that often benefit from individual intervention prior to joining a group include survivors of sexual abuse or other traumatic abuse, people with extreme social anxiety and those who are in fact suited for a group intervention but are very personally opposed to joining the group.

A good group therapist, however, recognises that group therapy is not always the right intervention for everybody; part of the job entails knowing when to refer individuals to a different sort of intervention.

Why the Needs ABC?

The client-centred approach of the Needs ABC, which helps clients to identify how their behaviour is causing them problems, and why they are drawn to certain behaviours, means that the outcome of therapy releases into society an individual who has become better able to negotiate her social relationships, while the integrated approach, combining cognitive-behavioural, motivational, client process, narrative and emotion-focused concepts, gives therapist and client alike a wide focus for the discussion, analysis and solution of problems.

Let's begin our exploration of why the Needs ABC works by looking briefly at the various components integral to its formation:

Cognitive-behavioural therapy

Cognitive-behavioural therapy, initially derived from the work of Albert Ellis[8] is based on the straightforward hypothesis that the emotions we experience stem from our beliefs, our interpretations, our evaluations and our reactions to the circumstances in which we find ourselves. Problems occur when stress arises as a result of irrational beliefs, interpretations, evaluations and reactions. The therapist's role, according to this approach, should be to aid the client in learning how they are reacting irrationally, to identify their triggers and to cease such unhelpful reactions. Ellis believed that emotional and behavioural difficulties arise when desires for, for example, love and success are experienced as urgent needs. The failure to provide oneself with these 'needs' can result in depression, anger and intolerance, depending on whether the associated negativity is turned inwards or outwards.

Motivational therapy

Motivational therapy is facilitated by utilising open-ended questions, affirmations, reflective listing and summarisation.[9] At its core lies the 'permission' embodied in the technique for the client to lead momentum as much as possible. The role of the therapist is to help clients by pointing to their strengths rather than their shortcomings, by listening carefully and respectfully to what they have to say and by providing them with their own insights about themselves and their behaviour in a succinct, easy-to-understand way. The goal is to lead the client towards change by prompting self-motivational statements that will precipitate new ways of responding to needs, while expressing empathy, supporting self-efficacy, 'rolling with' defensiveness rather than challenging it, and helping clients to perceive the discrepancies between what they need and what they currently have. Motivational interviewing involves helping the client to identification of certain advantages or benefits, and costs or disadvantages associated with a given behaviour, so that clients can make rational decisions on the basis of real criteria.

Narrative therapy

Narrative therapy, developed largely by Michael White, David Epson and the Houston Galveston Institute's[10] Harry Goolishian and Harlene Anderson, takes place in a philosophical environment in which individuals approach both therapy and being 'in the world.' This approach stresses the subjectivity of experience as it is created and experienced by people as they talk and interact with others and with themselves. According to this approach, human reality is created in a social context, through language and conversation, while generating both language and meaning. In the process of social interaction, individuals construct their own narrative, ascribing meaning to their experiences and the stories they tell about themselves and choosing certain words with which to describe their own experience. According to this view, individual's problems arise from 'oppressive' stories, which come to dominate their daily lives. Therapy occurs in deconstructing the client's use of language and the relationships they have created and in exploring multiple constructions of reality, providing the client with new ways of understanding his problems. The client's use of language and insights are key, with the therapist functioning as a facilitator.

Emotion-focused therapy

Emotion-focused therapy was formulated by Susan Johnson and Leslie Greenberg.[11] It combines the perspectives of attachment and structural systems theory, and focuses on the internal organisation of emotional experience, and how this is expressed and communicated. It assumes that human beings possess the innate need to connect to others, especially when they are in distress, and that attachment in childhood and adult relationships alike provides the security, comfort and contact that human individuals need. When these needs are not met, troubled behaviour develops in response. This approach maintains that most troublesome behaviours arise when the individual is not confident in receiving the security, comfort, etc., that she requires. In panic, she may attempt to bully or coerce those in significant relationships to provide her with what she needs. Of course, unpleasant behaviour such as violence, threats, sulking, etc., can only exacerbate the situation and does not successfully fulfil the unmet needs, creating yet more dysfunctional behaviour and aggravating the situation yet further.

In utilising this approach, the therapist acts as a mediator between the emotions behind the behaviours that are troublesome and the person who is experiencing these emotions, and coaches clients in more productive ways of expressing their emotional needs to the people they care about.

The Needs ABC's defining goals

Drawing on the above models, yet distinct from each, three important goals govern the Needs ABC:

- **Safety**: The facilitator should help the clients to connect to the setting and to the process of therapy. This helps participants to begin experiencing a sense of safety that can lead to greater participation and self-disclosure;
- **Ownership**: Once a sense of security has been developed, the next goal is for the client to take responsibility for his problem and collaborate with the leader and other participants in the development of appropriate strategies;
- **Understanding**: The facilitator should assess a client's emotional states during the therapeutic process and to help them understand what these emotions represent, and why and how they behave in the dysfunctional ways that they do.

Creating a healthy therapeutic setting begins with the first contact between client and therapist, and this is where we now turn.

2
A good therapist

WE HAVE ALREADY established that what distinguishes group therapy from other sorts of communal attempts to deal with problems is the presence of a suitably qualified individual who can engage a group of relationally unconnected individuals in the process of collaborative problem-solving, and who assumes responsibility for 'steering' the group in the direction it needs to go, and by providing insights that benefit from his or her knowledge of the precepts of psychotherapy. The same can be said of the professional who fills a similar role in the context of individual, couple or family therapy. But what are the specific qualities required of this person? In other words, what distinguishes them from the other people in the room?

The most basic prerequisites for Needs ABC leadership (and, I would argue, *any* effective therapeutic leadership role) are to like people, to have good social skills and to be properly trained. Each facilitator will, to some extent, redefine the role in terms of her own personality and style, but these three qualities should be constant. Other key elements are:

The possession of relevant qualifications

Various academic routes can provide individuals with the basic knowledge on which to build a future as an effective facilitator or leader, including having completed studies towards becoming a social worker, counsellor, psychologist, applied human scientist or other helping professional. Certainly, a high degree of insight and sensitivity towards others are prerequisite. However, less important than formal qualifications are other properties, such as the amount of clinical experience and practical training one has received, particularly hands-on training specific to the type of therapy that the facilitator intends to offer and a knowledge of various theories and perspectives vis a vis group, family, couple work etc. rather than just one model and the ability to be both flexible and integrative with these models rather than pre-emptive.

Awareness of the utility of life experience

One's personal life experience is also a valuable component, and a broad spectrum of experiences and interpersonal interactions with others is crucial as well as individual preparation and training in setting aside subjectivity so far as is possible, in order to be able to put oneself 'into other people's shoes.' Above all, one's sociability and general pleasure in the company of others are clearly a prerequisite in all forms of psychotherapy! As an aside, it is interesting, if not necessarily helpful, that many socially awkward people are also drawn to the helping professions! (Perhaps they are really looking for help for themselves.)

Facilitation skills

In a way, the term 'leader' is almost a misnomer, because the Needs ABC approach to group therapy really involves helping groups to lead themselves; assisting them in 'staying on track' and helping them, as individuals and as a microcosm of society, to find their own voice. Traditional models for group therapy derive much from the family-based model of patriarchal society, with the group leader as 'Dad' (whether the leader be a he or a she) and the group members as troubled children looking for guidance. Needs ABC is an offshoot of the social work group work approach, which is less authoritarian and based on mutual cooperation, both in group and in other forms of therapy.

The facilitator does not take the reins, but finds a way to hand the reins over to the people about whom the therapy should be; the group, family, couple or individual therapy participants themselves.

With this in mind, potential facilitators intending to utilise the Needs ABC model, as it is explained in this book, must learn to set aside ego, to listen, to prompt rather than command, to suggest rather than forcibly challenge and to empathise with and identify clients' emotional bases for maladaptive behaviours, rather than the behaviours themselves. This can, and frequently does, require working with people whose maladaptive behaviours are deeply unpleasant, even criminal at times, and impossible to condone in any context. But the role of the Needs ABC facilitator is not to condone or condemn, but to see the person rather than the behaviour, and help her to find a way to set aside her dysfunctional behaviour in exchange for a more productive way of engaging with the world in which she lives.

Awareness

If a group or other therapeutic unit is functioning well, the facilitator's voice is one of those heard less often. This is not to say, however, that he can ever relax and 'let the group get on with it.' Indeed, we will be looking later at some of the things that can go wrong when the facilitator does not intervene when it is appropriate to do so. The facilitator must listen, watch and learn. Being able to do so means becoming able to set aside many of our own prejudices and opinions, and learning how to see the world 'through others' eyes.' The Needs ABC leader does not just take words at face value, but considers them in the context of the information that the client has already believed, and in conjunction with body language, posture and changes in tone and voice modulation in the knowledge that the most important text embedded in the words the client chooses to use is often the least obvious one.

Objectivity

It has been argued that there is no such thing as complete objectivity, and this may be true, but Needs ABC facilitation does require that the group worker strive for objectivity so far as is possible. Particularly, it is important that she learn not to take setbacks or criticisms personally but as opportunities to explore issues with the individuals presenting for therapy. Of course, there will be times when she likes or dislikes someone strongly at 'gut' level. A group worker is, after all, a human being! The important thing, however, is not to let these likes or dislikes interfere with a proper, respectful treatment of the individual in particular and the therapeutic unit in general. Similarly, the facilitator's own views about 'good' careers, 'intelligent' interests and 'reasonable' religious and philosophical opinions are not generally relevant to the key issue at hand, which is helping a diverse group of people work together towards more healthy relationships with their world and the people in it. At bottom this means that if the therapist is, for example, devoutly religious or an ardent atheist, that's just fine – so long as he leaves these beliefs outside the door when therapy is ongoing.

Respect

Individuals attending therapy often tacitly lend their respect to the group leader until or unless he does something to lose this respect. The very least the facilitator can do is return this respect. Individuals presenting for therapy will generally recognise when they are being disrespected and this can have a profoundly negative impact on the likelihood that therapy will result in a good outcome for them.

Regardless of clients' level of education, political views, intellect, ethnicity, etcetera, a deeply felt appreciation of their common humanity and essential worth is crucial. Respect is signified to clients not just by respecting their views and culture but also by arriving at meetings on time and appropriately dressed (for example, a group of older people might appreciate a degree of formality in dress), applying courtesy to all interactions and informing group members in good time of any changes to the composition and scheduling affecting the therapeutic unit.

A model for group work and other psychotherapies

Fig. 1
Things are not always what they seem (gender-cultural)

Gender awareness

On a related note, it should be stressed that Needs ABC leadership requires an understanding and acceptance of changes in gender roles, and of the fluidity of gender-related behaviours that has always existed but that only recently has been widely accepted. As Mark Doel[12] says: 'At a theoretical level, the dominant postmodern paradigm suggests that notions of 'male' and 'female' are simplistic, and that the divisions and subgroups within these categories are considerable.'

While gender remains an important identity issue to many, perhaps most, neither men nor women are served well by a facilitator who clings to rigid notions of gender-appropriate behaviour. It is important to understand and appreciate that vulnerability, aggression, fear and abusiveness are not traits that are exclusive to one gender or the other but, instead, are present in varying proportions in all people of both genders. Neither sex benefits from assumptions that men should invariably behave in one way, and women in another. Men and women in therapy should feel free to broach and discuss emotions not stereotypically associated with their gender without fear of ridicule or criticism, especially from the therapist!

An understanding of cultural issues

The ·Needs ABC facilitator should have a good general understanding of the cultural biases of all the members of a group, including herself. There is no reason why a group cannot function well with members of both genders (with certain exceptions, as we will discuss) and from many different ethnic backgrounds. However, an awareness of potential biases allows these to be brought into the open, be discussed and become part of the therapy itself. For example, different ethnicities may be comfortable with different levels of disclosure about sexual feelings. While open discussion is a prerequisite of good therapy, different levels of disclosure may represent 'openness' to different people and it would be inappropriate and counterproductive to try to coerce clients to discussing in-depth issues that are, to them, intensely private. Frequently, working with people of different ethnicities is made easier by asking about and observing some simple cultural niceties, such as inquiring whether first names can be used, whether it is appropriate to greet with a 'hi' or a more formal handshake, and so forth. Overall, a useful, adage to observe is 'when in doubt, ask.' Exploring cultural differences between group members can at times provide a useful therapeutic tool in removing the emphasis of inquiry from the individual onto a less personalised general group. In the case of clients from ethnic minorities, the facilitator should be aware that these have to find a way to adapt their behaviours not just in light of their unmet needs, but also in the context of a culture different to their own. This may involve a certain amount of cultural brokerage, as the facilitator finds a golden mean between behaviour that is culturally and personally acceptable to them *and* to the host culture in which they have chosen to live.

Self-awareness

The ·Needs ABC facilitator should have a significant degree of self-awareness and the ability to disclose feelings honestly and authentically when this is appropriate. They should be able to draw on their own experiences of coming to a group, be it a therapy group, a study group, a committee meeting and so forth in order to understand such elementary emotions as initial nervousness, expectations of self and others, frustrations and perceptions relating to self and others, and feelings of support or otherwise.

While some facilitators will have been in therapy themselves at some point, possibly in the context of their training (a situation which many would view as ideal), having had a mentor in a less formal setting, such as a grandparent, teacher, close friend or relative, can also be effective in terms of understanding expectations and responsibility taking. Of course, all lives are different and a therapist will never have led the 'same' life as her clients. However, the ability to draw on 'parallel' experiences with the same emotional components as those experienced by the client is important. For example, the therapist who has not experienced sexual violence at the hands of a family member will never completely understand how it feels to the client who has had this experience, but the emotions of anger, sadness, shame and trust-breaking associated with other types of betrayal will be familiar and can aid in understanding and providing help. In this respect, it is essential that the facilitator become enabled to take a broad view of the emotions associated with specific problems.

Ability to stay on track

The facilitator should be able to keep on track in terms of maintaining focus on the emotions and specific topics under discussion rather than getting side-tracked by content. Staying on track also calls for the ability to supervise and to take back control from the group if and when this becomes appropriate. Conversely, when the group is on track, the facilitator should know when to 'keep out of it.'

Onward and upward

So much for what the therapist should expect of herself. We will explore the application of knowledge and skills, as well as the above-mentioned personal qualities, in the therapeutic setting throughout this book. But what should a client, who has made the all-important decision to seize the reins of their life, expect entering therapy? This crucial question brings us to the next chapter.

3
Creating a productive therapeutic setting

IT CAN BE difficult to trust an unfamiliar environment. Just think how a child feels on the first day at school, or an adult on entering a new workplace. It is not easy. One does not know one's parameters, and one feels uncertain about how to behave. This is even truer in the case of entering therapy, which has the clearly stated agenda of exploring feelings that make us unhappy, finding out how we are contributing to these negative feelings, and determining what we need to change about ourselves.

In order to create an arena of trust, the group work, family, couple or individual therapeutic environment should provide a supportive framework ensuring the emotional safety of the individual or individuals seeking help. The ·Needs ABC model focuses on the creation of a safe, predictable environment that makes sharing feelings easier for the participant and also reflects the sort of environment that they need and want to carve out for themselves in the wider world. In group work in particular, if they want (for example) to learn how to be able to talk with members of the opposite sex in a reasonable, unthreatening way, they can practice doing this within the boundaries of the group before bringing their newly learned skills to the wider world.

Practical issues in group work

Practical issues in group work include, but are not limited to, the number of participants or group size, the compatibility of members with regard to their ability to eventually participate and collaborate effectively, and the potential for destructive or harmful (both emotional and/or physical) behaviour to arise. When forming a group, one should bear in mind that it should not be too large or too small – it must be big enough to allow for adequate interaction between group members, but not so large that any participants are in danger of finding their voice lost in the crowd. The members who form the group should be broadly compatible in terms of what they need and what they can offer each other. While no two people have exactly the same problems, individuals who all share, for example, the loss of a loved one, will be better able to help each other than a group composed of people with radically different issues. Similarly, some participants do not belong together in group work for reasons that are quite obvious; female rape victims, for example, would not be well served by attending group therapy together with men who have problems with sustained violent behaviour towards women and vice versa. On the other hand, there is no reason why younger and older adults, women and men, more and less educated individuals and people from very different ethnic backgrounds cannot come together in a truly transformative way. In fact, a degree of 'difference' only serves to highlight the simple fact that is at the heart of the Needs ABC Model approach; that the core feelings, emotions and fears that bring most people to therapy are latent in us all.

Components

In brief, the components of the Needs ABC include:

- **the screening interview;**
- in the case of group work, **the group's phases** (sign-in, working phase, didactic phase and sign-out);
- the recognition of **client stages** (safety, social, inclusion, collaboration and continuity);
- **client pacing** through the use of 'supportive challenging.'

The details of all of the above will be discussed further as we progress, but we can summarise by stating that the Needs ABC strives to create and maintain an atmosphere of emotional safety for its clients from the initial contact (often over the phone), through the screening process, as well as from the client's first experience of therapy to the termination of treatment. Needs ABC facilitators work consistently towards maintaining a positive working relationship throughout by appreciating that there will be varying levels of client comfort during the therapeutic process and by employing interventions that 'read between the lines' of what their clients are saying (client narrative) in order to implement process theme based techniques that examine the client's emotional needs and globalise them to the group.

First impressions:
From the telephone to the screening interview

Although some writers on therapy consider first contact crucial to a client's eventual success in therapy, the issues surrounding the phone call and/or screening interview that generally comprises one's first therapeutic contact are surprisingly neglected in the literature not only of group therapy but also of other therapeutic approaches. Regardless of whether a prospective client is considering entering group or individual, family or couple work, we consider that the individual's therapy begins the moment she picks up the phone and calls to enrol in a group or another form of therapy. Remember that, for many, the decision to attend therapy is a very big one. The first big step towards meaningful improvement has been taken in acknowledging that there is a problem; many people never even get this far, and understanding that one has a problem is a major step forward that should be respected.

First client contact frequently occurs over the telephone, and even in a five minute conversation a facilitator can help to set the scene for effective future therapy. A good initial contact can help to promote client accountability, offer tactics for 'saving face' and suggest strategies to help the client to risk lowering defences. The first contact can introduce the client to a supportive structure that can help and encourage forward momentum at an appropriate pace.

First and foremost, one should recognise and respect that clients are often very nervous about making contact with a therapist. By discussing their qualms and expectations, they can be encouraged to understand that they have started their journey towards emotional wellness, because they, or somebody else, have recognised that they have a problem that requires help.[13] How their initial phone call or even email proceeds or is responded to can have long reaching consequences for their therapeutic experience. On the most immediate level, it is during the first contact that the therapist can ascertain what sort of therapy is right for them at the current time. For example, an individual who has suffered sexual abuse and is in need of counselling may need to work with a therapist on an individual level for some time prior to joining a group so that they can discuss what they need to address in a group context without feeling pressured or having difficult memories come up for them in group without warning. In fact, it is not uncommon for individuals suffering from various problems to benefit from some individual therapy before joining a group. Regardless of the sort of therapy the client is presenting for, the way in which their initial contact is responded to is key.[14]

For group therapy to be effective, one has to consider good intervention strategies from the moment of first contact, not just when the client comes to the group. For many, reaching the conclusion that they need help is a painful, challenging process that can necessitate looking long and hard at characteristics that seem to be central to their very identity as a human being, and making difficult decisions about changing or even eliminating certain aspects of the way that they have always been. Women and men alike may have to face the possibility that behaviours that they have always assumed to be appropriate for their gender are actually personal, and maladaptive (such as the woman who dissolves into tears at the slightest hint of conflict, or the man who resorts to violence). Parents may have to look long and hard at how they are raising their kids; spouses at their treatment of the person they love the most in the world; the lonely at what they are doing to drive others away. None of this is easy, to say the least. Still others may first come into contact with a group leader when they have learned that they must attend therapy for legal reasons, such as being able to obtain access to their own children or with the understanding that attending therapy may help to reduce their jail time. Some people have to attend therapy even as they are being punished for some transgression, and may be tempted to view the therapy as punitive also. Exploring painful issues, while a crucial step towards emotional wellness, involves rubbing a lot of salt in a lot of wounds.

However a client for therapy first joins a group or a therapeutic session, their first contact can be a very stressful moment and it must be dealt with great care; the adage that first impressions count for a lot is certainly true here.

Frequently made over the phone, starting therapy generally begins by scheduling a screening interview, so that the therapist can gain some understanding about why the individual needs therapy and what sort of intervention will work well for them. In the case of clients presenting for group therapy, it would be very foolish indeed to allow an individual to enter group therapy if they have not met a therapist (if not the therapist who will lead the group, as is ideal) in an interview context, as this is truly the only way to reasonably determine what is bringing them to therapy, what sort of group they are likely to function well in, and how to optimise the likelihood of a positive outcome to therapy.

The screening interview

The screening interview is a bit like a first date insofar as it sets the scene for an ongoing relationship between the client and the therapist. If a client is challenged too soon or too emphatically, they may go on to participate in group sessions or therapy with reluctance or with reservations, or not arrive at all. If the therapist jumps to conclusions about the client's situation, or does not really listen to what the client is saying – directly and indirectly – therapy may not start on the right footing, or the client may start therapy with a feeling of being intimidated.

The first client contact can be just as important as the first session in motivating and encouraging group work clients to take responsibility for their participation in the group. Where denial, minimisation, and fear can be significant obstacles to a client's treatment goals, the initial contact can help to promote client accountability, offer tactics for 'saving face' and suggest strategies to help the client to risk lowering her/his defences. In addition, the first contact can introduce the client to a supportive structure that can help and encourage forward movement at an appropriate pace.

Given just how important first contact is, it is surprising how little has actually been written about how to cope with a client in this setting! Unsurprisingly, first contact with a therapist is not a situation in which it is easy to be open and honest about one's problems, and it is common, if not typical, for individuals to be guarded, nervous and defensive. They may feel that in seeking therapy they are displaying weakness, worry that their problems make them seem abnormal or 'weird' and fear that the therapist will dismiss them or suggest that there is something gravely wrong with their way of being. All of the above is magnified in the case of those who are attending group or another form of therapy involuntarily. Even when meeting clients who present themselves willingly, however, one should not expect the absence of defensiveness about the very notion of therapy. We all know that emotions are complex, and even those who openly state that they require help may be resistant on other, deeper, levels. Knowing on an intellectual level that one needs help is not the same as feeling it.

Let's look at an example of a client presenting for a first screening with apparently deep-rooted ambivalence.

Example: Ethel

Ethel is a 41-year-old woman, married for the third time, with no children of her own. She has been a heavy drinker for many years, and although she is still attractive, the toll that alcohol abuse has taken on her health is very evident in her circled eyes, worn skin and general air of defeat. She is well-dressed and presentable, but beneath her cologne the stale smell of the habitual alcoholic is perceptible.

The first contact that Ethel has with her group therapist is by phone. She waits until the house is empty. She takes a shower and changes her clothes before calling. While she waits for the phone to be answered, she chews on a finger nail.

When the substance abuse intake counsellor answers and asks Ethel what she can do for her, Ethel's words come out so quickly that they seem to tumble over each other.

'It's my husband, Ted. He asked me to leave.'

'Why is that?'

'Well, I was hitting him. I'd had too much to drink. The kids started to cry. Then he said he'd had enough. I'm staying with my mother and he says he won't take me back until I sort myself out and stop drinking. In fact, he said it's even too late for that now.'

Originally from Britain, Ethel had come to Canada with her mother many years before. She describes her mother as 'selfish' and 'unsupportive,' even though it was to her mother's house she fled when Ted told her she must leave. Ted has filed for divorce and told her that if she wishes to see her stepchildren, of whom she is very fond, she will have to have counselling. Ted has told her that she is 'crazy' when she drinks hard liquor and that he doesn't want 'someone like that' around his kids.

Although Ethel agrees to enter treatment, she's bringing a lot of baggage with her. If she enters treatment, this will be her fourth time. She's seen someone about her alcoholism on three separate occasions, once before and twice after her marriage to Ted. On one of those occasions, she went after Ted presented her with an ultimatum. Now, at least on the surface, Ethel seems to really want to seek treatment. She has even enrolled with AA and has started to attend AA meetings on a regular basis. Now facing middle age, she seems to feel that it's 'make or break,' even if her physical and verbal abuse of Ted has destroyed her marriage.

'I know I have to change,' Ethel says. 'I've been in treatment groups before, but I realise that I have yet to change my attitude. What I continued to do didn't get me very far. I want to learn from my past mistakes and to own my behaviour.'

She pauses to take breath, and then adds: 'I'm also really depressed. I know I'm completely responsible for what's happened. I loved my husband very much and all I can think about is when we were one happy family. I come from a family where my father left my mother and my mother has basically humiliated me for forty one years. Ted is either away on work or doing stuff with his kids ... and now he's gone too. This group is my last resort. If I can't get help here I don't know what I'm going to do.'

What does Ethel's first contact with the therapist reveal? As well as Ethel's communication of her intent to seek help for her alcohol abuse problem, she reveals other issues. Clearly, she is frightened, not only of what will happen to her if she continues to drink but also of what will happen to her if she does not, and even of the therapy itself. Her testimony on the phone refers to everything in a deeply negative light, suggesting that her entrenched world-view is far from positive. Her internal testimony, if we may call it that, probably goes much like this:

I'm scared you won't believe me. I don't want to be punished. I've been punished and humiliated enough. What I really want is confirmation that I'm not a sick person and recognition that I have decided to get help. What if I can't succeed after finishing this treatment? Even if I am successful, I'm worried that no one will be able to see what I've accomplished. If no one can trust me, why should I even try?'

The counsellor's role at this point is not just to hear what Ethel is saying overtly, but also to understand, without jumping to conclusions 'set in stone,' what the messages embedded in her statements are. In other words, the counsellor must try to understand the underlying issues that are prompting Ethel's behaviour and bringing her to therapy. If the counsellor picks up on Ethel's apparent feelings of futility and fear, she may think:

'The prognosis for this client is rather poor since she's been in three previous

treatments. For her to have any chance at success this time would be a small miracle. As well, how can she even begin to limit set if she can't save her fights for when his kids aren't there? If I accept her into treatment, I am going to be held accountable ... and what if she fails again?'

If this is the counsellor's immediate reaction, a valuable opportunity to set the scene for real progress has been lost and the counsellor has fallen into the trap of filling the same role in Ethel's life as all the other people around her. Both the counsellor and Ethel herself are starting the therapeutic process with the assumption that it is not going to work out–a potential self-fulfilling prophecy if ever there was one.

However, there is another way of approaching Ethel's situation; one that keeps Ethel's needs and concerns at the heart of the counsellor's response. Let's take a look:

Preparation for a Screening Interview

Although Ethel's circumstances and outlook might appear bleak, if the intake counsellor takes a more optimistic and encouraging approach to her fears and anxieties, she may be enabled to take part more easily and actively in treatment. Rather than leaping to conclusions, the therapist must a cknowledge that Ethel's worries are not faulty but understandable and real, and look closely at what Ethel is saying so as to formulate ideas about ways in which Ethel might be able to meet the needs that are currently unmet and that are at the root of her behavioural problem and bad situation. By looking inside the text of Ethel's remarks, one can find a number of possible themes. In saying that her husband is often away on business and is not there for her, she may be expressing her feelings of emotional abandonment. When she describes her attempts at controlling her drinking and her relationship with her mother, it is probable that she is describing feelings of powerlessness in her life.

At this point, rather than discussing her alcoholism – a symptom of her malaise rather than the cause of it – the counsellor might make one of the following emotion-focused process theme statements:

I guess it is really frustrating when those you feel closest to keep running away; Or,

It must make you angry to think that so much of your life is out of control.

These non-judgmental statements recognise the disappointment Ethel feels at having little or no power over the degree of intimacy she needs from others. When Ethel says things like, 'I must learn from my mistakes,' and 'If I can't get help here, I don't know what I'll do,' she may be indicating her vulnerability to being exploited by others and her inability to know when and whom to trust. The therapist might acknowledge these feelings of apprehension in the following empathic way:

'Gosh, if I'd been through what you've been through, I'd be really scared and certainly wouldn't know when to let my guard down.'

Here the counsellor supports her lack of confidence rather than challenging it, belying her certainty that she must constantly be punished for speaking up. To Ethel's expressions of her inability to have a say in how her life should unfold, the counsellor could offer:

'I guess it must be pretty sad to feel that things never seem to go your way. It would sure make me angry at myself for not being able to understand how to get what I need.'

Here the counsellor has picked up on the possibility that some of the anger might be self-directed and has modelled appropriate self-disclosure. As well, it is an acknowledgement of Ethel's self-felt futility in the world and possible feelings of loneliness arising from her inability to trust people and to take charge of her own needs and emotions, which might account for her drinking problem.

It is, of course, always possible that the counsellor may not understand Ethel's underlying feelings completely. It is important that Ethel be given the opportunity to respond by correcting the counsellor's interpretations. For example, Ethel might say:

'Well, rather than scared I would say that I am angry...'

Towards the end of their first conversation, the counsellor's task is to leave the client with some feelings of optimism and encouragement to continue on to her next group work experience. In our example, the counsellor decided to summarise and validate Ethel's concerns in the following motivational way:

'You know, Ethel, it is impressive that, despite all odds, you are still not willing to throw in the towel. I know it is scary to think that you might

not succeed this time either, but your need to feel like a family member, included and needed, seems to have driven you to desperate attempts at getting your needs met. I am going to set up an appointment for an interview with Shirley. I think you will like her. I am sure she will understand how lonely and powerless you feel. I'm pretty sure that if we can help you to understand and clarify your emotional needs then you can help us to help you plan a better way to get them.'

By helping Ethel to consider a concrete goal that can be 'fine-tuned' as she moves along her next treatment path, she is more likely to feel optimistic and encouraged in her treatment experience. As well, by suggesting that she needs to be in charge of her own treatment she can begin to feel more empowered by using the treatment process as a metaphor for her life.

How a newcomer to a therapy group perceives the first therapist they encounter – the person doing the screening interview – has a big impact on how this client will engage in the treatment process and even whether or not they will stick with it at all.[15] The better the 'screening influence' is, the more likely the client will take part actively in treatment. This is also the time when clients should be told what to expect during the treatment process, especially when the screening interview is carried out by the person who will be heading the group, as is ideal.

Screening as therapy

The best way to view a screening interview is as the client's first therapy session. If the client is respected and listened to properly, a good initial contact can help them to take responsibility for their own therapy, even as it impacts on their views and feelings about their therapist and therapy in general. In short, it has a big influence on whether or not their therapy works out for them. Ideally, the person who does the screening interview is also the therapist whom the client will see when she has enrolled in a group. In Ethel's case, however, another group work counsellor is assigned to her case.

The counsellor is informed that Ethel seems to have high emotional needs for reassurance and validation of her experience as 'victim,' and that she seems to expect that the therapist and/or the group will eventually punish and humiliate her. Ethel's seemingly overwhelming situation could be based on her fear that she is an incapable and unlovable person, and that she is forever the victim of alienation. Ethel appears to feel that, no matter how hard she tries, she can't seem to get anyone's positive attention. As mentioned above, this view underlies several emotional themes, including her fear that she is not worthy of love for love's sake; that all her relationships are conditional, and that she can't do anything to change her life.

Even from an empathic point of view, many screeners might feel the need to challenge these fears and frustrations with statements like:

> 'I know it is horrible not to feel trusted, especially by those you love. I suppose if you could control your drinking things would have gone better for you.' or:

> 'Anyone would be angry at feeling abandoned the way you have, but I guess when you lost it in front of his children it was 'the last straw.''

On the surface, both of these interventions appear empathic and supportive. However, they also amplify the client's reality that she has been powerless to change the more shameful behaviours that she has displayed. This could reinforce her sense of discouragement and fear that she will be punished for her transgressions. For example, she might think:

> 'Even the counsellor thinks I'm bad! How could I have done what I did in front of those kids? Why can't I stop my drinking when I want to? Why am I even trying to get help ... again? I might as well just hang up now and forget about it.'

Helping the client to develop a sense of optimism is fundamental to any clinical interview, and is especially important in an evaluation for group work. A more optimistic intervention at this stage would be:

> 'I know it is horrible not to feel trusted, especially by those you love. I suppose that one of the things you could have the group help you with is how you could redevelop the trust in the other people that you need to keep close to you.' or:

> 'Anyone would be angry at feeling abandoned and powerless to do anything about it. Perhaps you could consider sharing this in group so that, together, you can figure out how to get some power back, rather than giving it up to drinking or your anger.'

In this way, the worker is offering Ethel an opportunity to take charge of her treatment by giving her some suggestions as to how she can begin her treatment, as well as some therapeutic goals she could aspire towards.

Many clients' perceived defensiveness to therapy and change – really a sense of apprehension or nervousness that can seem on the surface to be them 'digging their heels in' – springs from the anxiety they understandably feel when they think about all the changes they will have to make. This anxiety can lead to resentment about having to be in therapy in the first place. However, just as alcoholism is a symptom of an underlying problem rather than the problem itself, so is this apparent defensiveness symptomatic of anxiety, rather than vice versa. Apprehension can be exacerbated even further if the therapist mentally labels the client as being 'resistant' rather than 'apprehensive,' as is more typically the case. When the therapist understands that apparent defensiveness is the expression of a strongly felt anxiety, they can support the client in looking at things they can do to make things better. When the therapist invests attention and time in understanding their client's needs from the outset, rewards are reaped more easily as a result of therapy. It is important to understand that clients and therapists must work together towards the desired outcome for the client. Both must be prepared for the effort involved: The responsibility for the outcome of the therapy lies on the shoulders of client and therapist alike. The therapist's role will be to support and acknowledge the efforts and breakthroughs of the client, and the client's to become open to really looking at new ways of approaching the problems that have brought them to therapy.

When individual therapy is necessary before group meetings

While screening and evaluation can, with appropriate vigilance and attention to detail, set a client on course for a productive engagement in therapy with their group facilitator and other members of the group, another important task implicit in screening is to identify those individuals who may require some individual therapy prior to engaging with a group. People with psychiatric and/or depressive symptoms may need help bringing these under control with medication and/or individual treatment before joining a group, while individuals who will be bound to face traumatic memories – as in the case of the survivor of sexual abuse – may need to discuss their therapeutic needs individually before therapy so that they are not shocked into a sudden, unprepared-for confrontation with memories and traumas that they are not yet ready to deal with. While groups offer many benefits to a wide range of clients, especially in terms of socialisation, collaborative problem-solving and reality testing, the intensity of stimulation and emotional involvement can be excessively trying for those with very anti-social personalities. Determining when group therapy is contraindicated, and when it should only come following a course of medication and/or individual therapy should be an intrinsic element of the screening process.

Getting the ball rolling: First group encounters

In any new group, people will experience anxiety, diffidence and a reluctance to engage with other members. The role of the group facilitator at this point must be to introduce people to one another, and help them begin to talk about the relational difficulties that have brought them to therapy in the first place. It is important to appreciate that it is completely normal for people to have doubts and concerns in any new situation, and even more so in the context of a group in which they feel they will be expected to lay their souls bare. The group facilitator should, therefore, endeavour to help everyone feel as secure with the situation as possible on the first encounter, while not losing sight of the fact that, as the group continues to meet, difficult, uncomfortable and painful topics will have to be broached. The key achievements that the facilitator should work towards in the early stages of a group are summarised by Wickham[16] as follows:

- To establish a safe, but not necessarily comfortable, working environment for the treatment process;
- To clearly demonstrate what is to be accomplished and how the work of the group is to be accomplished; and
- To demonstrate competence in his or her ability to lead the group through each phase of development.

Throughout therapy but especially during the delicate early stages of a group, the facilitator should remember that her key function is what Yalom refers to as the 'instillation of hope.'[17] The hope that is referred to here is the realistic hope that dysfunctional behaviour can be eliminated and a more healthful way of dealing with emotions assumed in its place. It is during the first few meetings of a group that the scene is set for a successful therapeutic outcome for all the various members of the group. In 'open' groups in particular, in which new clients enter and 'old' clients leave on an ongoing basis, the first few sessions a client attends can literally make or break the outcome of therapy.

Helping a group to form the Needs ABC way

For the group leader to create a successful group from a 'bunch' of strangers, he should be able to perform as the notional leader of the group, while observing the qualities that make him as a Needs ABC facilitator. In this respect, a number of guidelines provide focus:

- Group workers are often concerned as to how active or passive they should be. Determining an appropriate stance involves helping group members view the facilitator in a positive light, and helping them to engage fully in the therapeutic process;

- Knowing when to say nothing or very little is just as important as knowing when to speak up;

- Maintaining a degree of structure in holding meetings is helpful in providing a sense of place and a feeling of security. It is useful for group members to know that, each time they attend a group, they will go through a series of procedures – signing in, greeting members, etcetera – that will aid the transition from 'normal life' to 'group';

- The group leader should remember that her role is to facilitate group members in making links with other members, in forging relationships and in coming to their own conclusions about why their behaviour is dysfunctional and what they need to do to make it right;

- All group members have a right to speak and to be listened to. When a group 'leans' too much in favour of one or more dominant members, the whole group suffers.

- So far as is possible, questions and comments, by both client and leader, should be generalised to the group;

- The group leader should be prepared to reveal information about themselves when this seems appropriate; when modelling their own behaviour can help group members verbalise something about themselves;

- The group leader should be prepared to help the group stay on focus, rather than drifting off-topic or falling into the trap of attacking one of its members in an attempt to deflect an uncomfortable issue. A certain amount of deviation from the core discussion themes of the group can be revealing of personality and other aspects of group members, but the leader should know when to gently steer the topic back to the subject at hand;

- Understanding emotions – those expressed directly, those hinted at 'between the lines' and those unexpressed – is key. Verbal utterances and physical expressions of discomfort should always (if not always obviously) be observed and analysed by the group leader;

- Emotions and themes should be generalised to the group, even when they are caused by different personal circumstances.

Maintaining a group

While inevitably a group facilitator is the focus of a new group, as time passes and the group develops its own personality and momentum, her role should be to disengage from an overt leadership role as group norms and dynamics emerge, so long as these norms and dynamics are reasonable and constructive. If the group seems to be developing the norm of scapegoating an unpopular member, for example, the facilitator will need to step in and break this cycle of destructive behaviour.

All groups have a culture of their own, operating within the wider culture that is the society in which the group's members live. This is true of groups of children at play, of religious congregations, hockey teams, immigrant communities and union members. It is also true of groups of people who have come together for therapy, regardless of how diverse their life situations are. As time passes, and especially in the earlier stages of a group, 'cultural' norms are tacitly agreed upon. These norms will become the conversational 'rules' of the group and whether or not they are consistent with self-disclosure and honest discussion will have a great impact on the viability of the group as a therapeutic entity. It is during the early period of a group's meeting that these norms are decided; mostly as part of the process of a group's evolvement, but some in a deliberate 'policy-making' way. In 'open' groups, the group culture is more variable and prone to shift and change as members join and leave the group, but despite this ebb and flow of accepted norms, the same ground rules of striving to be reasonable and constructive apply.

While assisting the group to establish healthy norms that will allow for a free flow of discussion and give voice to all the components of the group, the role of the facilitator should be to support the themes under discussion and, so far as possible, to allow the group to interact in a reasonably free manner, although there will be times when intervention is necessary, in order to allow all group members to speak and take part in the session. As Yalom[18] puts it:

> The group facilitator's task in the group is to help members understand that they are the movie. If they do not perform, the screen is blank; there is no performance.

Always remember that people come to therapy because they find it difficult to give their emotional problems a 'voice.' Group therapy helps them to find that voice – but only if they are allowed to speak! The facilitator can help with this process by finding links between topics under discussion and topics previously discussed, by pointing out common themes shared by various group members, by deflecting tension if and when it arises and by gently helping a useful group dynamic to emerge while maintaining focus on the specific reasons why the various individuals have come to therapy in the first place.

In doing so, it may at times be appropriate for the facilitator to reveal something of himself in order to model self-disclosure. This can take the form of empathising vocally about a problem that group members have. For example, the facilitator could share some of the feelings he experienced on the loss of a loved one or how he sometimes feels frustrated and annoyed by his spouse's or sibling's behaviour. By demonstrating that he considers the group to be a safe place in which to share something of himself, he opens the field to group members to do likewise. If the therapist maintains a lofty, god-like role in the eyes of the group, he is likely to find that his 'feet of clay' are exposed, whereas if he shows his common humanity unashamedly, the knowledge and interpretative skills he possesses are more likely to be accepted by the various members of the group.

4
The Needs ABC Model in practice

ALTHOUGH EVERYONE'S CIRCUMSTANCES are different from everyone else's, fundamentally human beings are more similar than they are different. There are many biological and evolutionary reasons why this is the case, but this is not the right place to explore this fascinating topic. Instead, it is profoundly liberating to understand that, regardless of our age, family situation, educational or social background, gender or ethnicity, our emotions and the way in which we can sometimes react to these emotions in a less than productive way, are also experienced by others. No matter how complex our emotional geography, we are never alone in experiencing it.

That said, the process of therapy can be a difficult one, and many clients will find it over-bearing at times, especially if they feel that they will have to confront issues that they have been avoiding. Clients demonstrate this reluctance by defocusing from the topic at hand, externalising the issue through rationalisation, blaming others, using 'we' or 'they' instead of 'me' or 'I,' and by generally attempting to distance themselves from the situation at hand. The challenge for group facilitators is to help group participants become more resilient, so that they can choose alternative, more functional problem-solving strategies within and without the context of the group and on to the greater world in which they live, work and play.

The Needs ABC approach to therapy is broad-ranging, and integrates various different therapeutic approaches to combine client, therapist, contextual, and environmental process with motivational, narrative, and emotion-focused work. The core assumption of the model is that 'bad' or maladaptive behaviour is displayed by people because they are attempting, however unsuccessfully, to fulfil unmet emotional needs. Needing something – a 'needs-deficit' that is not provided – creates an uncomfortable feeling, and the maladaptive behaviour (be it excessive drinking, drug abuse, violence, or whatever) results from poorly-thought-out or completely reflexive attempts to eliminate the discomfort.

In therapy, the challenge that faces therapist and client alike is to find out what the unmet need is, explore how it relates to qualities missing in the relationships that the client has with other people, or themselves for that matter, to examine the feelings this brings up for the client, and to look at ways in which the deficit can be met. For example, if a man consistently responds to his partner's requests for help in the house by yelling and punching the wall, it may be that her requests remind him of a stressful situation he endured with his parents throughout childhood. In not understanding that, in consequence, he needs to have his limits respected and should broach this topic with his wife in a calm and rational manner, he responds with a storm of unreasonable behaviour intended on some level to 'solve' this unmet need, but failing absolutely. Understanding the needs and behaviour formed in childhood does not excuse the man's maladaptive behaviour, or offer him license to continue with it, but it does explain it to him, which in turn makes it easier for him to learn to deal with his unmet needs in a different, more productive way.

Recognising the commonality of experience, and identifying a number of finite ways in which unfulfilled needs are experienced provides us with a template for helping people who are apparently very different recognise what they have in common and how they can come together constructively. The Needs ABC is strongly focussed on the universality of experience. In practical terms, this means that, rather than providing one-on-one counselling in a group setting, the counsellor's role is to involve all the members of the group in discussing the unmet needs of each group member, to relate to their experience and to collaborate in enabling members to break out of the loop that they have been stuck in for once and for all.

A topic that will be touched upon throughout this book, but that is worth underlining here is that much emotional experience is truly universally held. Clearly, there are differences in the way we all experience the world, and some of these differences are linked to issues of ethnic and gender identity. However, these differences tend to reside more in the details than in the broader scope of felt emotion. A wider focus enables us all to understand that many emotional experiences can be understood and related to by others.

The Needs ABC 'hangs' on four crucial practice techniques that are essential to supporting participants in a successful group work experience:

A model for group work and other psychotherapies

- the awareness of **client process** in both individual contact and group sessions;
- the understanding of **group process;**
- the identification and exploration of **universal themes** descriptive of missing relational needs for the group as a whole and for individual group members;
- the recognition of the **emotional components** of a client's narrative.

Interpretations formulated from these techniques, when reflected back to the client and, as an observation, to the group, can support the development of possibilities for clients to meet their group work goals. When applied respectfully, these skills can become the 'royal road' to the identification of client relational needs.

Rather than focusing on just the content of a client's narrative, it is important to focus on the 'universal theme' – 'universal,' because of the ease with which it can be related to by other members of the group – embedded in it. This enables client and therapist to work together to uncover the client's unmet needs, and to strive towards finding a more productive way of dealing with them than has been the case to date. For example, a man might focus on his frustration at being 'stood up' by his partner by saying:

> 'She's always late for everything and is very disorganised with everybody. I can't even trust her with the children since I never know when she will be available.'

This expression of frustration reflects the client's feelings of powerlessness, and the fact that he currently feels that he must accept his partner on her terms, and fears having to martyr himself to the relationship.

Instead of focusing on the 'problems' per se – which would seem in this case to be a lack of assertiveness and apparent difficulty with limit-setting – the facilitator could support the therapeutic unit in examining what the client needs from his partner (his relational 'needs-deficit') so as to improve his emotional safety. Taking this 'universalised' approach eliminates the risk of diminishing the client's self-esteem, by taking the personal and making it general. In group therapy, an approach like this moves the group from suggesting that the client is 'frustrated because he does not know how to get his partner to listen to what he wants' to the more helpful proposition that his 'frustration stems from the fact that his wife does not acknowledge his needs in the relationship' and that he is 'angry that he is feeling 'marginalised' by her.'

If the client accepts his need to 'feel acknowledged and important,' he can address this need in a more focused way both within and without the relationship. By helping him to identify areas of his life in which he is recognised and validated – at work, for example, or with his softball team – he can begin feeling more independent. This increased independence will, in turn, make it easier for him to challenge his partner about what he needs from their relationship, in a non-confrontational way.

Another example of how a group can work with the individual could be when a member of a single parents' group begins to reflect on how he finally understands that he was responsible for his marriage break-up and that his behaviour caused an irreversible rift. At this point, other members might 'jump in' to defocus from, or dilute, the emotional significance of what is being said by suggesting, for example, that his partner could also have done more to help the relationship. With the facilitator's help, the group members could then move to exploring their own issues of perceived abandonment and alternative strategies for dealing with this relational concern.

Group process/client process

Group process is, as Yalom puts it, 'the nature of the relationship between two interacting individuals.' [19] In other words, in group therapy, group process refers to the way in which the group members interact with each other and with the group facilitator. However, it is not limited to the words they use or the statements that they are making on the surface but rather the intent and secondary meaning of the words and the way in which these are reacted to by other members of the group. Group process has been described by Garvin (1974) as the vehicle by which social skills and appropriate behaviours in relationships are modelled and assimilated.

The Needs ABC defines group process as the way in which the group develops in terms of cohesion and interpersonal dynamics. Client process is defined as the way in which a client expresses her interrelational needs; needs that were usually formed during childhood (we will be discussing the 'latency' period below). These are generally expressed in terms of the universal themes that will be discussed in considerable detail later in this book. When the client starts to express these needs differently, we consider that a change in process has occurred and that this, in turn, means that a change in the client, or 'movement' has taken place. In plain English, it is a question of practice making perfect. Group process refers to the way in which members of a therapy group use their interactions with each other to acquire the social skills that their emotional problems have been preventing them from practicing, while client process is the way in which clients verbally express the psychological shifts that are occurring within them, and helping them move towards a more productive way of being part of society. In any group, the members tend to pass through a specific series of stages. In the context of utilising the ·Needs ABC approach to therapy, these can be described according to the McGill Model, which was developed by this author:

The incoming client stages: The McGill Model

Many models for doing group work are based on a stage theory that, in describing group process, also identifies stages that clients should pass through in order to get the most from their group experience. For example, the classic five-stage Boston[20] lists as group stages 'pre-affiliation, power and control, intimacy, differentiation and separation, while Bruce Tuckman's model describes group members as 'forming, storming, norming and performing in groups.'[21] The Toronto Model[22] and the Windsor Model[23] have beginning, middle and end stages. Schiller[24] has described her stage model to reflect critical aspects of group work with women suggesting that strengthening relationships, inclusion, and interpersonal empathy are important when working with women.

The McGill model, crucial to the Needs ABC approach, was developed[25] by this author at McGill University, from which it takes its name. The Needs ABC believes that more appropriate labels will support a more empathic and optimistic stance in the person responsible for running the group and are described as follows:

1. The 'safety' stage

When an individual joins a group, they are usually apprehensive about what membership of the group will mean to them. It is difficult for them to trust the other members and the therapist, even if the screening experience has been a positive one. They may doubt their own ability to gain enough confidence in the group and themselves so as to be able to benefit from therapy, and this concern can give rise to fear, anger, ambivalence or all of the above. Group facilitators

Fig 2.
Incoming client stages I: The 'safety' phase

can promote a feeling of safety within the group by modelling self-disclosure and encouraging group members to do likewise.

On entering a group for the first time, the therapist heads straight to make herself a cup of tea or coffee at the refreshment table. 'I don't know about you guys,' she says, 'but I always find it easier to meet new people over a cup of tea and a cookie!' Several of the new group members chuckle and also help themselves to cookies, agreeing that sharing a warm drink and a cookie can help to break the ice. Enjoying a warm drink on a cold evening is something that everyone can relate to.

When new members join an open group, extant members can show them, through their words and their actions, that the group is a safe place in which to disclose information about themselves, as in the following case of a man who has been ordered to join a group to address his violent treatment of his wife:

> John (to new member): 'You remind me of when I first came here. I was really pissed off. Now I know I was just afraid that I would be hammered out for doing what I did to my wife. But hey. We're all coming from the same place here. You might find that you're with people on the same wave length for the first time in a long time!'

When self-disclosure is modelled in such a way, newcomers to a group often respond by reducing their defensiveness, showing that they are more comfortable and feel safer about being in the group:

> Antonio: 'Yeah, I am pissed off. Who wants to spend football season stuck in a room talking about your so-called problems? I suppose I'll get used to it. After all, you guys are here for the same thing, and you've been sticking it out for a while now, right?'

The group process also profits; such an empathic interaction models the style of relational work that is central to the purpose and dynamic of group therapy.

2. The 'social' stage

Fig 3.
Incoming client stages II: The 'social' phase

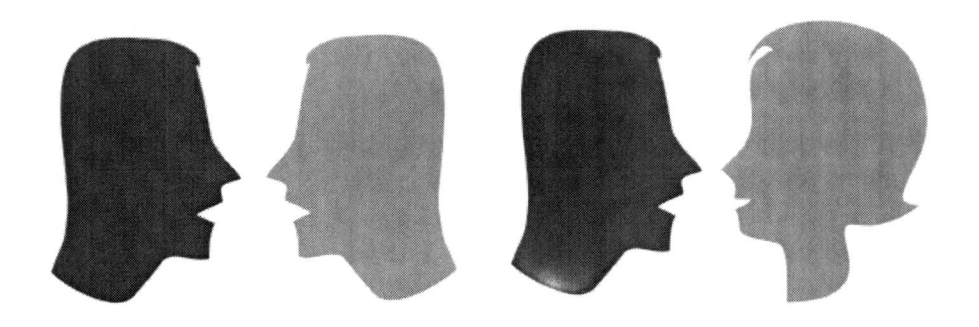

The second phase of group process involves the establishment of a relational base. People who attend group therapy need a forum in which to learn the social skills that they are lacking. By learning how to relate to the other people in the group, they are enabled to start doing this. An incrementally improved ability to relate socially to others in the group enhances self-esteem and communication skills and provides tools for better social relationships in the wider world. This may sound straightforward, but while the rewards are great, the process can be a tortuous one. Individuals with difficulties in communicating with others may attempt to reach out to others socially, even as the words they choose indicate cynicism, rejection and anger. For example, when a woman says, 'Nobody in this group has any idea what I am going through,' her intention may be to communicate: 'I am afraid that my problems are so uniquely horrible that I am anxious about disclosing them, much as I would like to.'

Because of their anxieties relating to social interaction, group members may attempt to adopt clearly defined roles: 'the bossy one,' 'the victim,' 'the disliked member,' and so forth. While these roles may provide them with social cues that enable them to speak, as the group process develops, it is important to move beyond the confines of these clearly defined, limiting roles towards a more balanced interaction with the group. Let's explore an example:

Example: Anne

Anne has a friendly demeanour. She often discusses her experiences, remarking, *'You think you've had it rough, but you should take a look at me. I was sent to prison for 12 years while my friend got off scot-free. I don't know an easy way of doing anything.'*

George assumes the role of group reporter, and 'interviews' his co-members as if he were preparing an article, asking questions like, *'Do you think it is possible for an addict to really become "normal" once he has crossed that line?'* and *'Do you think you can identify core traits of a typical addict?'*

Jacques assumes the role of co-therapist by saying, *'What do you think is the thing that most often pushes your buttons?'*

At face value, one might assume that these roles are not of much therapeutic value, as they do not seem to reveal much of the inner life of the speaker. However, they do make it possible for the members of the group to start interacting, and this is the foundation of successful group therapy. A problem will arise only if group members remain constrained within the roles that they have chosen for themselves.

3. The 'inclusion' stage

Fig 4.
Incoming client stages III: The 'inclusion' phase

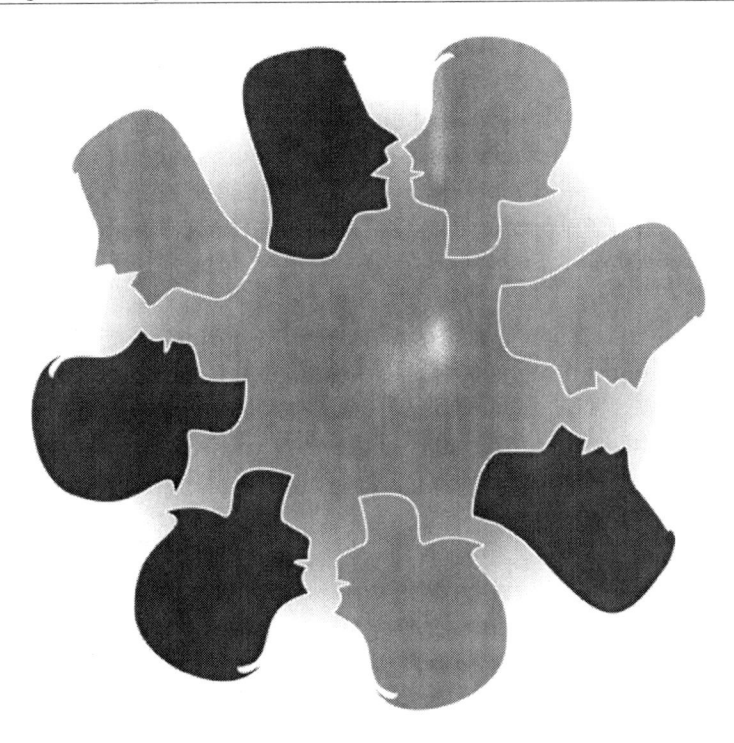

When a new client feels reasonably comfortable in a group setting, he begins to be able to reveal more of himself, and start moving away from a 'fixed' role. This can happen when he has already had the opportunity to see others opening up about themselves. He may think, 'If she can do it, so can I.' He starts to behave less defensively, and effectively enters the group process. In response, other members of the group frequently encourage this client to speak out by being empathetic, and validating his stance, tacitly recognising that he is trying to adopt a new role in the group. For example, a client who has not yet entered group process might say:

> 'I'm having a great week. I know now that I'm never going to be violent again. Now whenever my wife and I have an argument we sit down and talk it out. I'm really glad I came here.' Or,

'It is important to set limits with yourself. Hitting a woman is wrong. You can't blame her for being angry with you.'

Rather than revealing his inner life, the speaker is presenting an idealised version of his experience. As he moves towards a more active stance, he will become able to risk more self-disclosure. For example, he might say:

'It was a good week. This is one of the few weeks that I felt I really wanted to come in. I am constantly worried that I might relapse. I hope it isn't always going to be this much work. I had a situation come up this week, and I'm not sure if I handled it as well as I could have. I wonder if I could get some feedback from the group?'

In response to a client's self-disclosure, the group tends to create an atmosphere of commitment to the issues at hand, and a greater sense of community spirit. When one person becomes able to open up, it strengthens everyone's confidence in the capacity of the group process to help them, too. In response to the comments above, a fellow group member might say something along the lines of:

'It is good to hear you're making progress, Rob. I think I am too. But I bet it is normal to feel concerned about a relapse. I get really impatient sometimes, and just wish I could move beyond this whole thing – but I know we all need to pitch in and help out. What happened to you this week?'

4. The 'collaboration' stage

We refer to 'collaboration' as a situation whereby group members work actively together to help each other become enabled to function better in the wider world. More established members of the group help less confident or newer members. Most group members have begun to experience how changes in their behaviour are impacting on their relationships and life experience and are acquiring skills in communication and self-disclosure. For example, in a group meeting about the issue of alcohol abuse, the following dialogue might be heard:

Anne: 'Boy, when the winter starts to close in, I find it a lot harder not to drink. The evenings are so much longer and it's so depressing outside it makes a bar seem a whole lot more appealing. It's hard to walk past the bright lights and music and know there's nothing to look forward to but a

A model for group work and other psychotherapies

Fig 5.
Incoming client stages IV: The 'collaboration' phase

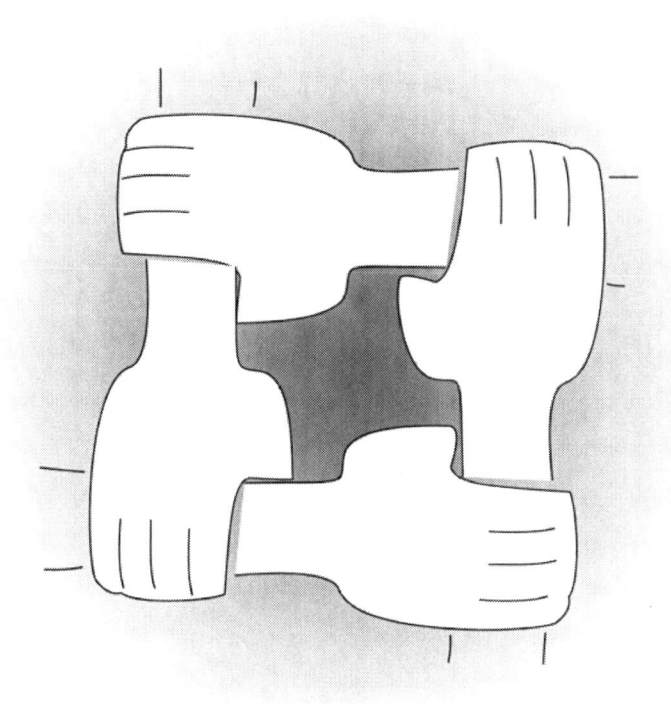

long night in front of the TV. It makes me feel that everyone else is in the frame and I'm on the outside, looking in.'

George: *'Yeah, I know what you mean. I often feel the same way but I try to offer myself an alternative treat like going to the movies or ordering Chinese. It helps to take away the craving.'*

Anne: *'Yes, that might help. But I think it's also because Christmas is coming, and that reminds me of how lonely I am sometimes.'*

Charles: *'That makes sense. I bet most of us know what a challenge Christmas can be. I won't even start in on my in-laws (laughs). But still, there are lots of things you could do when you feel like drinking, just like George says.'*

5. The 'continuity' stage

Fig 6.
Incoming client stages V: The 'continuity' phase

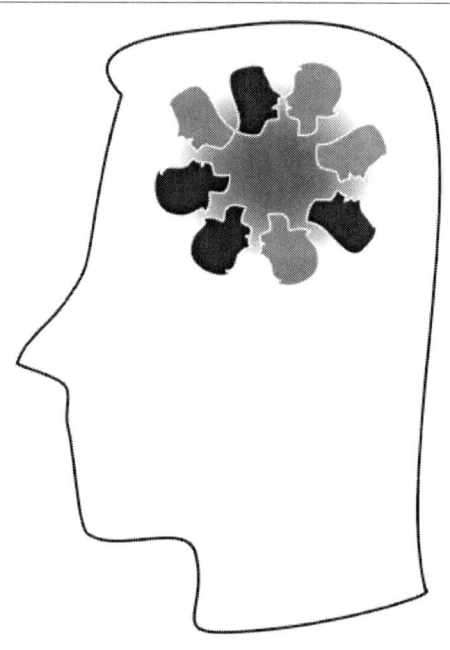

When a client feels ready to leave a group, he often states that the best teachings of the group have been incorporated within himself. Clients can also use the review of their personal growth in treatment to launch them into advocacy in the world outside of the group. Specifically, the client can now approach intimate relationships with the same emotional openness and reciprocity that he has discovered works in the group:

Example: Matthew

Matthew, a recovering substance abuser whose issues included feelings of 'not measuring up' to his partner's expectations, stated that he had learned from the group that criticism does not necessarily imply defectiveness. Now, when he suspects that his wife is being critical he is able to examine with her whether this is a lack of competency on his part or simply 'a matter of preference.' His feedback has been that it is usually the latter and that this has helped him to be 'less hard on himself' and to avoid 'drinking away his 'poor me's.'

A model for group work and other psychotherapies

The usefulness of co-facilitation and therapist teams

One of the issues that commonly needs to be addressed in group therapy is the way in which women and men interact in our society. Almost all of us have significant relationships with people of the other gender; spouses, parents, siblings, colleagues, friends. The way in which we view gender, gender roles in society and sexuality all impact very significantly on the way in which these relationships take place. Very frequently, problems arise specifically with respect to the way we respond to members of the other sex in our lives, especially spouses, partners, and potential partners. It seems to be easier to objectify members of the other sex, to generalise about their behaviours and motivations and to use frustrations inside ourselves as springboards from which to launch a series of unhelpful behaviours.

While the role of the group facilitator is to strive towards as high a degree of objectivity as possible, it would be disingenuous in the extreme for group therapists to suppose that their gender will go unnoticed by the members of the group that they are leading! For this reason, there are times when it is very helpful for a group to be facilitated by a woman and a man, or by a therapist who is the same sex as the members of the group. For example, in groups addressing problems arising from power struggles in personal relationships, group members may find it easier to disclose information about themselves following appropriate modelling from a facilitator of the same sex as themselves, while learning to be able to trust members of the other gender can take place in gradually becoming able to talk about intimate and distressing subjects with a group leader who belongs to a different gender. When members of a group are addressing subjects that can lead to tension and people becoming 'highly strung,' the presence of two group leaders can deflect taut emotions by allowing each to play a slightly different role. Let's have a look at how this can work in context:

Example: Alex and Bridget

Alex and Bridget share the responsibility for facilitating a substance abuse treatment group composed of both men and women. Today, group member Alyssia is recounting the multiple episodes of abuse she suffered at the hands of her partners, especially when she was stoned or high.

Emotions run high and finally a red-faced Alyssia turns on Alex, whom she has cast as the token 'male in a position of power.'

'You're all the bloody same,' she says in a raised tone. 'You men. Why can't you just keep it in your pants?'

Before Alex has had time to respond, John, who has admitted to suffering sexual abuse in his childhood intervenes: 'I am sick and tired of women thinking that they are the only ones who have it hard! It's worse for us men. At least our culture lets them whine and complain. We're supposed to be the strong ones, no matter what happens. When we are hurt or upset, we get called wimps. Women can just sit around and wait for someone else to pick up the pieces.'

At this point, Bridget interjects, saying: 'It seems that both men and women in this group can relate to how impotent they have felt in trying to protect themselves when they have been with individuals they were supposed to be able to trust.'

'Yes,' Alyssia agrees. 'I'm sorry, John. I'm not angry with you. It just all gets to be too much sometimes.' John nods in response to her apology.

Addressing the group, Alex remarks: *'Whether or not we could have made better choices is one thing, but trusting others seems to be a difficult thing for many of us. Maybe we can all think about this a little, and see what we come up with.'*

In this exchange, Bridget has reflected on the theme of 'powerlessness' that can lead to ineffective problem-solving strategies, whereas Alex has picked up on the theme of 'loyalty,' both of which may be very relevant to the situations facing the various members of the group. Additionally, Alex might feel more strongly about the theme of 'loyalty' versus 'powerlessness' and respectfully suggest:

'You know Bridget, I agree that lack of power in the world is a possibility, but I really feel that thinking you can trust someone only to have them turn on you is a much more powerful issue for some of the people here.'

Here Alex models an appropriate way to disagree with a group member or, in this case, a group facilitator, or bring in an alternate possibility. Without highlighting Alyssia's outburst, the group has been offered a new template for expressing conflicting views. It would be foolish, however, to suggest that co-facilitation is always this easy. As Yalom[26] says:

The disadvantages of the co-therapy format flow from problems in the relationship between the two co-therapists. It is important that they feel comfortable and open with each other. They must learn to exploit each other's strengths: One leader may be more able to nurture and support and the other more able to confront and tolerate anger. If the co-therapists are competitive and pursue their own star interpretations rather than support a line of inquiry the other has begun, then the group will be distracted and unsettled.

Of course, not all co-facilitation teams have to be mixed sex. Co-facilitation can also work well with two male or two female therapists. The strength of the mixed sex team, as Yalom[27] points out, is that, among other advantages, the dyad can 'strongly evoke' the image of the group as family, and help group members focus on problems they may have on communicating with various people of the opposite gender. In other situations, however, two men or two women fill a useful role.

Despite the many potential benefits of co-facilitation, many agencies offering group or other psychotherapies do not offer this option. The primary reason for this is generally economic; two salaries need to be paid rather than just one. Different clinics also tend to reach different decisions with respect to the appropriateness or otherwise of co-facilitation, often for reasons that are at least partly political. For example, in many cases group therapy for women victims of domestic violence are co-facilitated by two women rather than a man and a woman.

Closed vs. open groups

The Needs ABC model can be applied to both open and closed groups. The term 'open group' refers to groups without fixed beginning and ending points, with group members beginning and leaving therapy in their own time while 'closed' groups meet for a specific period of time, and cater to the needs of a finite, discrete number of clients. Neither one type nor the other is 'better'; each presents with certain challenges and advantages, and each can provide the best clinical environment given certain circumstances.

Open groups tend to meet for very extended periods of time, and have clients entering and leaving the group as they individually become ready to start and terminate treatment. Clearly, this can be quite challenging for the group facilitator, who has to juggle the needs of clients who are still uncertain about how to approach treatment and engage with the group with those of clients who are beginning to reach the stage of thinking about moving on. On the other hand, the group has some distinct advantages. Clients who have already made considerable progress with their therapy are in an excellent position to model effective disclosure to newcomers, while for those who are just beginning to come to terms with the fact that they need help with their own dysfunctional behaviours are encouraged and motivated when they see more established members of the group make meaningful progress and even 'graduate' from therapy.

Closed groups are run for a fixed number of clients over a fixed period of time, and in terms of organisation seem at first glance to be easier to run. Certainly, it is easier to plan for sessions. However, they also involve their own particular set of challenges. The group dynamic is a more rigid one, and the clients are more likely, without effective intervention on the part of the therapist, to find themselves falling into specific roles that may hinder their progress. If the therapist feels herself under pressure from any agency or other source to stick to a curriculum, this is also more likely to present problems to the closed group, with its more rigid format; it can be just that much too tempting to try to stick to prescribed topics for each session. A further challenge is that client process does not occur at uniform rates, and while some members of the group may be ready to move on from therapy when the group terminates, others may not yet be ready and may have to consider continuing with another group, and compare themselves unfavourably with their 'groupmates.'

Group and client process in action

Of course, none of the above is meaningful unless we can apply it in a useful way to real situations. Let's look at an example of how the process works from the viewpoint of a group therapy client:

Example: Ginger

Ginger is a young man, twenty years old, who recently dropped out of university where he had been rather half-heartedly attempting to follow an architecture course. The only son of parents who had him late in life, he lives alone with his father, who is already over seventy years old and quite frail following a series of strokes. Ginger's mother died suddenly when he was twelve years old, and his father retired at sixty because of ill-health and the pressure of raising Ginger on his own.

Although he is very bright, Ginger is by his own admission unable to 'stick to anything' and he is still financially dependent on his father. Ginger has come to therapy following an incident in which he pushed his father, knocking him over and causing him to break a rib when he glanced off the side of the table. Ginger is full of remorse about the incident, but is angry about attending the group, which he is doing under a degree of coercion from his father's younger sisters, who have told him that they will make sure his father 'throws him out' unless Ginger attends an anger management group. Ginger dreads any of his peers finding out that he is attending a group at all, and finds it almost impossible to verbalise his problems.

It is not until another, older, member of the closed group opens up about a violent argument that he had with his sister that Ginger responds by blurting out 'That's just like what happened to me!'

When he describes the argument with his father, the other group members agree with him that his behaviour was appalling, but also state that they can empathise with how dreadful he feels about having hurt someone he cares about very much.

As the following weeks unfold, Ginger becomes gradually more confident about speaking out. Little by little, his fears about having to deal with adulthood are vocalised, as well as his fear about his father dying: 'What would I do without him?' Another member of the group, Antoine, suggests that Ginger is afraid to finish college or 'sort himself out' because that might mean having to leave his elderly father. By staying in the position of dependent child – by questioning his competence – Ginger is showing that he still needs his father, and that the latter must therefore stay strong for him. He also dreads his father becoming so physically disabled that he cannot take care of himself and thinks: 'What is the point of doing well, if I will have to come home to take care of Dad anyway?' Finally, Ginger states that he thinks he hit his father because of feelings of being marginalised and his anger about being 'held back' by his situation. This disclosure is accepted by the group as likely, and several of the group members tell Ginger that, regardless of how frail his father is, he should 'go out and get a job' because he 'isn't doing his father any favours.'

This practical, almost harsh, advice is taken on board by Ginger, who applies for, and gets, a job at a local video store. It's not a great job, but having his own income enhances his self-confidence and his feelings about being 'held back' dissipate. Ginger becomes able to discuss his situation rationally with his father, apologise for his violent behaviour and discuss ways in which the two can help each other get on with their lives.

Here, key to Ginger's being able to find practical solutions to practical dilemmas as well as becoming enabled to vocalise his feelings about his situation is the fact that other members of the group were able to relate to his feelings and offer constructive input on the basis of their own experience. On the face of it, this might be a little surprising. Antoine, mentioned above, is a sixty-two year old, semi-retired, electrical engineer; and, other members of the group include Jim, a fifty year old auto mechanic of Somali origin, and Sam, a thirty year old CEO of a financial management firm specialising in providing services to Mandarin speakers. None appear to have very much in common with Ginger, the bright underachiever.

The following case study provides us with an example of client process in an open group setting:

Case study: Sharon

Sharon has been mandated to therapy to help her deal with underlying emotional issues thought to be related to her poor parenting skills. Her children are currently being cared for by a sister-in-law after having been taken from Sharon by social services. Sharon had not been actively abusing her children, but Jake and Rachel, two and three years old, had been identified by carers at their preschool as showing evidence of malnourishment and possible abuse. A follow-up visit to Sharon's home found the children alone while Sharon drank in a bar down the road. Medical examinations revealed both children to be underweight for their age, to be infested with lice, and to be manifestly unclean.

Sharon is initially resentful at joining the group, which has been meeting for a period of approximately two years, and which caters to parents of both sexes. She has also been told that she must attend a parenting skills course. During the first few sessions that Sharon attends, she remains on the fringes of the group, saying very little but appearing to listen with care to what is being said. The fourth session is also a final session for one of the group members, Paul.

> '*I never thought that this day would come,*' says Paul, addressing the group. '*When they sent me here, I thought "That's it. I've lost them now. I've lost my kids and it's my own stupid fault. I thought it would be a complete waste of time. I thought that a piece of me had just died off when my wife left me and that that was why I was such a bad father. Now I know that I am not a bad person, even if I was not. I understand things better now. I know I was responsible for screwing things up but I'm not beating myself up about it anymore, just looking forward to the future."*

The following week, Sharon addresses the group at some length for the first time.

> '*I know I'm just starting out,*' she says. '*But I was really encouraged by what Paul said, last week. Obviously I have a problem, but I have started to deal with it and that's good, right? I guess if I stick with it eventually I will be able to take care of my kids again and that is what matters here.*'

Challenging, linking and inclusion techniques

Various techniques, combined with emotion-focused, theme-oriented strategies, can be effective in helping group members to clarify and prioritise their needs and move towards more effective problem-solving. These are:

Supportive challenging

Supportive challenging asks group work clients to think about their ineffective or inappropriate ideas and behaviours without attacking their personalities. For example, June, a pregnant woman mandated by her physician to a substance abuse treatment group, might share the following information:

> '*I know I have to take care of my unborn child but I am still angry that my doctor forced me to come to treatment. I know I've slipped up a little, but I'm not an idiot! All I have to do is tell my friends that I can't drink. I don't understand why my doctor doesn't understand I have good friends who wouldn't want to hurt me.*'

Needs ABC: Acquisition and Behaviour Change

The group facilitator could supportively challenge June with the following observation:

> 'It's no fun to feel pushed around. It must be difficult for June to realise how out of control her life has been until now and how scary it must be to feel that she might not have the tools to keep herself safe when she leaves here.'

In this intervention, the group leader has recognised June's feeling of having little influence over herself or others and has brought it to the group in a general way, to encourage clients to relate to the theme of powerlessness rather than the specifics of June's story. Clearly, the specifics – being out of control and pregnant – are unlikely to apply to all of the other members in the group, especially as June's group is mixed sex. However, feelings of resentment at being 'told what to do' masking fears that one is not able to stay in control are likely to be shared by most people who have been sent for group therapy for substance addiction.

The endorsement of facilitators and clients' modelling appropriate behaviours and options for problem-solving[28] is a significant distinguishing characteristic of group work since, for many, appropriate interactions, self-disclosure and reciprocity have seldom been experienced in relationships beyond the group. Indeed, this is the core problem that brings a lot of people to therapy in the first place! A male peer group member (Fred) might enter the group discussion as follows:

> 'Yeah, I hate when people tell me what to do! It really ticks me off even more when I know they're right. I tried to ask my wife not to drink when I'm around but I soon realised that it was not her problem. Why shouldn't she have a glass of wine if she wants on? She never drinks to excess. I was the one who had to take responsibility for my addiction. I had to leave the room if I saw her pouring a drink ... I even had to go to a meeting once.'

Here, Fred is modelling appropriate self-disclosure for June as well as helping her to recognise her problem from a different perspective by sharing his problem-solving strategy. In other words, by disclosing information about his own difficulties and how he is learning to cope with them, he is providing her with a template for disclosure. In this case, June does respond to Fred's disclosure by shrugging, smiling wryly and saying:

> 'Yeah, I know the doctor's right. It's just difficult to listen to someone who doesn't really know what I've been through – after all, she's a successful

professional and she's always had it easy. She doesn't come from the wrong side of the tracks, like me. She's not like my friends who really care about me, and have been through so much with me. It's not comfortable facing the truth, but I guess I'll have to if I'm going to get through this O.K.'

Mentoring

Mentoring by clients with more group experience to other group members, in a supportive and productive manner, is more powerful and less intimidating than if it is done by the group leader. While the group leader cannot 'force' group members to mentor to each other, it is important to foster an environment in which mentoring can take place.

Jeannie, a cocaine addict who has been in several treatments and has had her children placed in care because the last was diagnosed at birth as having cocaine in her system, stated:

'Listening to you guys makes me feel very uncomfortable. People are always telling me what to do. What makes me sick is that I am really pissed off at myself for setting myself up. I know that I shouldn't use when I'm pregnant but I can't say 'no' to my boyfriend. I finally decided to leave him. As close as you think your friends are, the reality is that [pointing emphatically to herself] the 'buck stops here.' I don't know if I will be successful this time, but I do know that it will be easier doing it on my own for myself.'

Jeannie reinforces Fred's statements about the importance of taking responsibility for one's problems. In addition, because she also is a woman, and pregnant, she may be 'heard' by June more easily. Finally, with what seems to be an authentic piece of self-disclosure, she counsels June to take a more active role in her predicament. Already more receptive to the idea of change, June pats her 'bump' and says:

'Yes. And it's not just me I've got to think about. There's Junior here, as well. If, God forbid, he was born with any health problems and it was my fault, I'd never forgive myself. Ultimately, I'm the only one who can take care of us both.'

Linking and inclusion

By using techniques that focus on *linking* and *inclusion*, group members with apparently similar needs can be brought together by identifying process themes and their emotional components. Clients with dissimilar needs can also be asked to reflect on what they hear others commenting on and, in this way, can be linked to the group process. Clients can be 'linked' either to selected group members, or to the group as a whole. In the context of a group dealing with clients who have problems around substance abuse, after hearing what three members – June, Fred and Jeannie – had to say, the group leader remembered that Bradley, a relatively quiet, withdrawn member, had said that, in most relationships, he acquiesced to his partner but was never able to get his partner to give in to his needs. In response, the facilitator observed:

> 'I was reminded of what Bradley said last week about his difficulty with limit-setting around his needs with others. It sure sounds similar to what we're discussing today. [Looking at Bradley] I am sure Bradley can relate to what June, Jeannie and Fred have been discussing.'

By highlighting to Bradley his feeling of powerlessness in relationships, and the fact that others have felt the same way, the facilitator helps him to engage in group discussion. He also makes it easier for other group members to interact with or mentor to Bradley. In this case, Bradley shifts in his chair, clears his throat and says:

> 'Uh, yeah. Well, of course I've never been pregnant, as June as, but when it comes to having difficulty knowing when to stand up and take responsibility for myself, I'm definitely right there alongside June!'

Group linking

Group linking refers to when the facilitator 'throws out' an observed theme, or themes, to help the members of the group find common ground and bond with one another. Rather than focusing on Bradley, the facilitator could say:

> 'After hearing Jeannie, Fred and June, I was reminded of what Bradley said last week about his difficulty with limit-setting around his needs with others. I wonder if anyone remembers his predicament. It sure sounds similar to what we're discussing today.'

Here, the facilitator has generalised the concept of relational impotence to the group, enabling members to recognise the theme of powerlessness in their own experience, and bond with other members who are having the same realisation. In this case, the various members of the group can verbally recall what Bradley said the previous week and its relevance to the discussion at hand.

Client-paced work

One way to help clients feel in control and able to be open is to recognise their expertise in the subject at hand. This also makes it easier for the facilitator to **pace** the client effectively and to collaborate with them in exploring various ways to problem solve, and choose one. In order to help clients feel in charge of their treatment process, the·Needs ABC group work model promotes *client-paced* work. Work is done at the client's rather than the facilitator's pace in order to help everyone in the therapeutic unit assimilate their problem-solving strategies and meet the goals that have brought them to therapy. At its most simple, this approach is based on hearing what the clients, and not the facilitator, deem important. Let's take a look at some dialogue from a support group for adults in a centre treating individuals with eating disorders:

> Facilitator: 'Today our topic is 'limit-setting.' Perhaps during the sign-in you each can reflect on what the term means to you and how your successes or failures in this area have impacted upon your relationships with the people in your lives.'
>
> Terri (who has just turned 18): 'I am sick and tired of hearing about limits! Ever since I came here, people have been telling me what to do. Who cares if I go to bed after the curfew? I'm not in anyone's way. It really sucks having to pack up and leave when I'm watching a TV show and I want to know how it all works out. People keep telling me to behave like an adult, but then they treat me like a baby.'
>
> Elaine (a mother of 3): 'Terri's right. Some of the rules are stupid. Why do I have to go to all the therapy sessions – can't I skip one or two? I need time for myself you know…it's more healthy. Yesterday I got in trouble because I ran myself a bubble bath instead of turning up. But I knew I just needed to relax on my own!'
>
> Lisa (a divorcee with adult children): 'Rules are made to be followed and I

> think in a treatment centre they are really important so that everyone can feel safe and able to work together. Imagine this place if everyone did what they wanted! It would be a real mess!'

A superficial reading of the above might give the impression that the clients of the centre had gone off-focus and attempted to change the topic at hand. However, the facilitator recognised a connection between the clients' statements and the context of the environment in which they are being offered therapy. Essentially, all the women were describing their need for a respite from coercion in their relationships as well as a need to feel both important ('marginalisation') and empowered ('powerlessness'). In response, the facilitator made the following process theme based, emotion-focused, statement:

> 'I guess we all get angry at feeling forced to do things we don't want to and treated as if our opinions don't count. I am sure most of you have plans to change this once you leave the centre.'

Universalising the clients' emotional reality, while supportively challenging the group's problem focus, allowed clients to describe some possibilities for acknowledgement and empowerment after moving on from the centre. Regardless of age, social class, gender or ethnicity, common feelings, fears and anxieties bind us together in an experiential continuum that spans all of the above categories. This is formed by what I refer to as the 'universal themes,' and this is where we shall turn next.

5
Introducing the 'universal themes'

THE TERM 'UNIVERSAL THEMES' refers to the common themes that can be identified in a wide range of client populations, that are 'universally' understood – that can be expressed using a simple emotional vocabulary that everybody will understand – and are the group facilitator's most useful tool in furthering the work of the group as a whole, and the progress of the group members as individuals. The term 'universal' should not be read as an implication that the themes below represent a discrete list, but understood to imply the common nature of the feelings described; these are issues that everybody can and will understand, like the physical qualities of hunger and thirst. Understanding what universal themes are and the multiplicity of ways in which they can be expressed through words and behaviours is central to the implementation of the Needs ABC approach to therapy.

Universal themes are themes that seem to express the way the client sees the world in general (world-view or 'client process'). These are emotionally (rather than rationally) based and often express unresolved issues 'left over' from the client's earlier development – usually in the 'latency' stage of development, which we discuss below. They are also 'universal,' insofar as they can be expressed in terms that are readily understood and identified with by others, representing, as they do, relational needs and the emotions that they provoke, that many people experience at some point in their lives and that result from the unique experiences each person lives through in the course of their childhood. The way in which these themes are expressed in the client's vocabulary and/or in their behaviours, dysfunctional or otherwise, will be influenced by issues including culture, gender, age and situation, but the themes *per se* are independent of these factors. Universal themes define and provide us with the vocabulary to discuss what is lacking relationally for the client in the world (needs deficit) – and what they have been trying to get (need) unsuccessfully. These universal themes, which represent the underlying issues addressed most frequently in therapy, are central to the understanding and practice of the Needs ABC, which has as a central premise the understanding that need drives emotion, and emotion drives behaviour.

The themes that follow were developed by the author and his colleague, Harle Thomas, in the course of their clinical work in areas including substance abuse, general anger management, gambling and domestic violence, with therapeutic units including couples and families. Both found that, regardless of the specific problem at hand, certain themes tended to emerge from therapy consistently, although somewhat different vocabularies could be used to describe what were essentially the same underlying issues.

It is not suggested here that the list that follows is a closed set of emotional themes, or that an attempt should be made to 'reduce' every issue to one of the themes listed below. Instead, each therapist may find that she needs to create her own list of underlying themes, depending on the issues she addresses. The universal themes listed below are a starting point that any therapist can use in initiating their own Needs ABC informed approach to therapy.

It should also be noted that the client-specific themes and emotions that they imply are not necessarily mutually exclusive. The landscape of human emotion is multi-layered and complex. More than one theme and/or emotion can co-exist; e.g. 'fear' and 'anger' or 'loyalty' and 'abandonment.'

Briefly, our starting point of universal themes and the way in which they are expressed, both derived from this author's experience, are as follows:

- **Abandonment**
  Fear: 'Here today and gone tomorrow.'
  Need for emotional reliability, predictability and consistency.

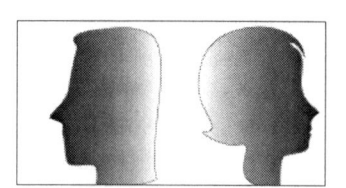

- **Loyalty**
  Fear of being taken advantage of or betrayal.
  A need to trust in others' motives and for unconditional support.

A model for group work and other psychotherapies

- **Intimacy (Closeness/Distance)**
  Fear of too much or too little space.
  Need for emotional connectedness.

- **Respect**
  Fear of being invisible or marginalised.
  Need to feel valued and acknowledged.

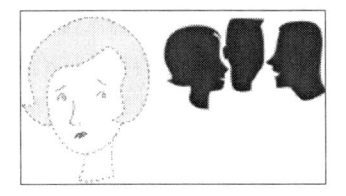

- **Competence**
  Fear of taking on responsibility because of potential to fail.
  Need to feel adequate.

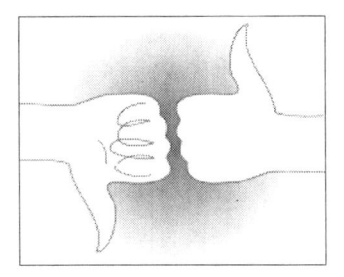

- **Power (to get needs met)**
  Fear of impotence and powerlessness.
  Need to feel in control of one's environment.

- **Grief/Loss (a 'Time-Out')**
  Fear of change.
  Need to accept finality.

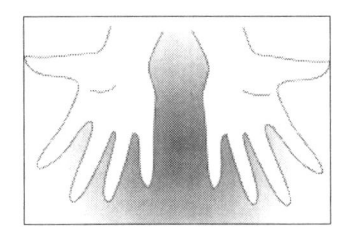

Instead of focusing on the specific problematic behavioural symptoms experienced by clients, it is more productive for therapeutic work to focus on the underlying themes and emotions that can easily be understood and discussed in productive, non-judgemental terms, always bearing in mind that emotions emerge from themes, and that emotions are what fuel and drive behaviour.

Individual experience is unique, but the range of emotions commonly experienced is finite (although not necessarily encapsulated here), so referring to universal themes will make it immeasurably easier for clients in group work in particular – but also in other forms of therapy – to relate to one another's situations. Differences of class, age, income and more disappear and are replaced by the remarkable parity of emotional needs and the limited vocabulary usually used in describing them.

For example, in the case of a group meeting to deal with problems relating to substance abuse, the reasons behind the problem may be manifold: ongoing distress relating to abuse in childhood, compulsive disorders, problematic relationships, etc., and each client might have different relational needs, but the themes and emotions associated with these unique experiences – fear of abandonment, a feeling of loss of power, and so forth – can readily be identified with.

Family of origin/latency

To stress the seminal importance of the family of origin is not to say that one cannot move away from teachings received in childhood, but simply that one should never underestimate the significance of upbringing on the adult person or attempt to dismiss problems originating in childhood with a statement such as 'it's time to move on from that now,' or 'but that was a long time ago, and has nothing to do with where you are right now.'

It cannot be too strongly stated that the relational dynamics in one's family of origin are crucial in forming the adult self. Even though coping strategies can emerge prior to latency, because of the absence of autonomy and mobility, those that emerge during latency are more recognisable and, often, can become the basis of the dysfunctional behaviours that clients bring to treatment. Parents teach their children, implicitly as well as overtly, how they should behave in relation to others, 'appropriate' gender behaviour, how adults relate to each other in the context of a marriage or other significant relationship and how to negotiate challenges such as work, the use or abuse of alcohol and other

Fig 7. Latency

substances and more. Everything they do is observed and can be replicated in their children's own adult lives.

Childhood is when both body and mind of the individual are formed, and anything that happens in childhood continues to reverberate throughout each person's experience of adulthood. Just as the adult knee still bears the scar caused by a toddler falling off a tricycle, so does emotional experience continue to shape our behaviour and reactions in both positive and negative ways in adulthood. A distant parent, problems at school or with authority figures or a feeling of not being taken seriously enough as a child all continue to form our behaviour as we continue to interact with the other people in our lives.

Although they may not have used the language of psychotherapy, when the Jesuits said, 'Give me a child until the age of seven and I will give you the man,' they were tapping into a very important truth; although we all grow up, the child we were remains with us always, and the adult we become retains the impressions, opinions and problems experienced in childhood, for good or ill. Each year we live merely adds a layer of experience to a personality that has been there for as long as we can remember.

Needs ABC: Acquisition and Behaviour Change

Human beings are social by nature, and that sociability kicks in from the moment of birth. Long before our ancestors even became what we now refer to as Homo Sapiens, they survived and continued to evolve thanks in large part to the complex social relationships that enabled them to hunt collaboratively, share childcare, and create communities. Even just after birth, when its eyes can only focus within a distance of about twenty centimetres, an infant likes to gaze at a human face so much that it can be 'tricked' into gazing at a schematic face drawn on a piece of card. These early attempts to engage their mother in an exchange of gazes represent the first of a lifetime of social experiences that begins at the moment of leaving the womb.

Bonding with other human beings in significant relationships of various types is fundamental to the human condition and the instinct that babies and children have to bond with their own parents and family members is as strong as their drive to eat, except in the case of children with disabilities such as serious autism, or difficulties relating to emotional deprivation in childhood. Children who have suffered a lack of human contact in their very early months and years – such as children in overstaffed orphanages, or infants who have had to spend a great deal of time in hospital – are very likely to develop emotional problems as they grow up, and in fact often 'fail to thrive' physically, even when they are receiving adequate nutrition and exercise.

Throughout childhood, our most important relationships are with our parents and family members, and it is from them that we learn to be members of society, members of our family and, indeed, fully fledged members of the human race.

The term 'latency period' was originally coined by Sigmund Freud[29] as denoting the period between the age of about six and adolescence when the libido appears to be repressed, and when the child's experiences are dominated by the act of learning what it is to be a member of society, both in the context of formal education and in observing those around him. The same term is used by Anna Freud[30]. Erik Erikson covers similar ground in his discussion of developmental states and tasks[31]. Erikson maintains that the periods he refers to as 'preschooler' and 'school-age child' are marked by the suppression of instinctive urges so that the individual can attend to the business of learning in school, with peers and with the various people he encounters in daily life. Erikson adds that this is a period in which the child is vulnerable to developing a deep-rooted sense of inferiority.

In my clinical experience, people typically come to therapy to deal with their maladaptive behaviours that seem to have their origin in childhood, and especially in the latency period – after early childhood and before adolescence – which is characterised by the child moving away from the instinct-driven behaviour of infancy and toddlerhood and actively seeking

A model for group work and other psychotherapies

to learn how to negotiate the maze of relationships that is our world. These behavioural strategies always seem to reflect the 'survival skills' clients have used in their earlier stages of development.

In childhood, almost all of our needs are met or thwarted in the context of the family, and in later years, society and our own social circles are felt, experienced and – above all – reacted to as a macrocosm of the mini-society comprised by the family. We can generalise by saying that the things that upset us in childhood, and especially during the period of latency – the unmet needs we experienced – will continue to be important issues in adulthood, and the adult person will strive to form relationships with people who appear to meet the needs that have gone unmet for so long. If our relationships with the significant others in our lives continue to leave the longed-for needs unmet, increasingly desperate attempts will be made to reacquire them, using the behavioural tools that were developed in childhood, or a version of them. The more desperately felt these needs are, the more effort is expended in trying to find them. If attempts as an adult to fill one's needs are thwarted, the adult individual typically resorts to strategies he used with some success as a child. For example, a child who was always the centre of attention, and who maintained this status by acting out ('throwing a tantrum'), would want to feel important (theme: respect) in his relationships as an adult. If he feels he is losing the attention he so desperately craves, he will try to recapture his place and may 'act out' in order to do so (for example, by engaging in domestic violence, substance abuse, etc.). The adult who had experienced an ambivalent or absent relationship with parents as a child would similarly act out.

For example, consider the man whose father abandoned the family when he was six years old and whose mother had to work two jobs to support the family, becoming less available (theme: abandonment, respect or loyalty). If his partner appears to be less connected to him than he would like, he will connect his present situation to his past and react accordingly, often with behaviour that is seriously dysfunctional and damaging to himself and others.

It should be stressed that, while people who grew up in abusive or seriously dysfunctional families often need therapy in later life, even those of us who grew up in generally happy, reasonably affluent circumstances can reach adulthood with unmet needs that continue to impact on our behaviour in a less than helpful way. In tandem, feelings and emotion-driven behaviour learned in the past and situations in the present can combine to create a painfully difficult emotional landscape, disabling the adult individual from being able to take an objective stance with regard to problem-solving and frequently resulting in immature, maladaptive responses that aggravate the situation further.

Cultural difference/human sameness

It is important to be aware of culturally informed behaviours in utilising the Needs ABC approach. While human beings are much more similar than they are different, regardless of the cultural chasms that might seem to exist between them, different ethnicities tend to discuss emotions in different ways, and a high degree of sensitivity to this issue is important. At their most basic, emotions of joy and sorrow are expressed in ways that are purely instinctive. Even children who are born blind will respond to a pleasant sensation or experience with a smile, and even children who are born deaf will wail when they are upset. As we all grow up and become encultured, these simple, instinctive responses are overlaid with more complex emotional reactions and with specific vocabularies and behaviours that are considered acceptable by the culture in question. Of course, discussing every possible ethnically-informed variation on descriptors for emotion is not possible, but exploring one example of how culture can impact on expression will be useful in highlighting how a failure to recognise the validity of culturally-informed responses different to one's own can lead to difficulties.

Perhaps one of the most striking areas of difference between cultures is found in the expression of grief in the event of the death of a loved one. When a parent, child, or sibling dies, profound grief and mourning generally follow. However, different cultures have developed different ways of processing these painful emotions. Some consider it inappropriate or even unlucky to talk about their feelings of loss. Others 'let it all hang out' and feel that they can cry and mourn openly, while yet others use formal expressions of grief and loss to discuss the pain that they are feeling. Some might even engage in behaviours that would normally be considered aberrant or odd, such as becoming very drunk, rubbing ashes into the hair, or foregoing washing for a prescribed period of time. The variations are endless. My point is that the emotions behind this infinity of behaviours are essentially the same.

None of the possible approaches to dealing with bereavement is necessarily wrong. Even usually destructive behaviours like drunkenness can be valid ways of expressing grief provided they occur in a formulaic 'for a special occasion' manner, rather than chronically. While the therapist may find it easier to identify with clients from her own or a more similar than different ethnic group, she will also have to be careful not to misinterpret the signals that she is receiving from other clients. Formal language, if its encoded meaning cannot be fully understood, may be difficult to interpret and could lead to misunderstanding and frustration.

Without wishing to understate the difficulties that can be posed by a group

A model for group work and other psychotherapies

composed of various different ethnicities, often simply asking about clients' ethnic backgrounds can be not just informative but also offer the opportunity to engage therapeutically.

Continuing with our example of bereavement, let's look at how a therapist might deal with her need to balance the needs of an ethnically mixed group:

Example: Bereavement group

Jeanne is facilitating a closed group meeting to discuss issues around the loss of a child. The group caters to a mixed urban population, and is composed of six individuals, as follows:

Sean, an Irishman in his fifties who moved to Vancouver shortly after graduating from college. Sean's twenty-eight-year-old daughter recently died in a traffic accident.

Mary-Kate, who is thirty, was born and raised in Canada. Her five year old son died of leukaemia last year after a brief period of illness.

Rajneesh, thirty-four and originally from India, lost his eight-year-old daughter to meningitis three years ago.

Benjamin, forty, from the United Kingdom, is half way through a three year engineering contract in Canada. His fifteen year old son died in a traffic accident eighteen months ago.

Angela, thirty-six, is Mexican. Her profoundly disabled toddler died when her life-support machine was turned off.

Franco, forty-five, is Italian, but has been living in North America for twenty-five years. His son, a professional diver, died last year off the coast of Florida. His body has never been discovered.

The group has met three times already, and is now discussing how they coped with the first anniversary of their child's death. Angela and Franco have spoken about how they visited their child's grave and wept. Sean and Rajneesh have spoken about how they found comfort in observing their respective religions' rites for the first anniversary of bereavement. Mary Kate says that, while she herself is not particularly religious, she also found comfort in observing the rites of her family, most of whom are Jewish.

When Benjamin is asked how he observed the anniversary of his son's death, he remarks that you have to get on with life, saying, *'There is no point in dwelling in the past, really, is there? I mean you just have to live your life and get on.'*

Angela finds Benjamin's remarks distasteful. She is already in a state of some distress and now she raises her voice and speaks angrily.

'It really doesn't sound like you cared about your son at all!' she says loudly. 'What kind of a father doesn't do anything for the anniversary? I have never heard of anything of the sort. This is ridiculous!'

Far from getting angry, Benjamin seems to become ever more withdrawn. His face becomes pale and he notably avoids 'catching the eye' of anyone in the group. Eventually, he says in a quiet voice, *'In my family, we don't believe in making a fuss. Jakie is gone and doing silly things isn't going to make things any better. Of course I remember the day he died, but on the anniversary I just went to the office and got on with my work. I needed to keep my mind off it.'*

The rest of the group and therapist – who probably should have deflected attention from Angela's verbal assault on Benjamin by now – need to understand that, even if Benjamin's culture and religious background do not provide him with rites to mark the anniversary of his son's death, and even if he feels that emotional language is inappropriate, this does not mean that his feelings of loss are any less profound. Without forcing Benjamin beyond a realm of expression that he finds personally acceptable, he should be allowed to talk about his grief in a way that he finds as unthreatening as possible.

Jeanne, herself of French-Canadian descent, is of a similar age to Benjamin and also has a teenaged child. Drawing on her own experience and emotions as a mother, she says,

'It must be very painful thinking of how Jakie died before he could grow up and make his ambitions come to life. I think that many parents who have lost a teenaged child ask themselves questions like, "Would he have had his first girlfriend by now?" and "I wonder if he would have decided what he wanted to do at university."'

'Yes,' Benjamin agrees. 'Of course, one asks oneself all those questions. And what is so difficult is that the answers will never be given. There's nothing left but questions now.'

Without attempting to force Benjamin to use a vocabulary that makes him feel uncomfortable, Jeanne has helped him to engage with the group and take further steps towards vocalising his grief. At a later point, a group discussion about cultural differences in mourning behaviours may be useful. Jeanne can also consider examining some of the group members' relational needs, as well as their issues around grief and loss. For example, when the time is right, Angela might need to explore issues around competency or loyalty, given her experience of having had to make decisions about her child, while he was on life support. Benjamin might benefit from working around feelings of powerlessness or abandonment.

Different themes can lie behind similar behaviours

Different themes can lie behind similar behaviours Universal themes can unite people apparently requiring therapy for maladaptive behaviours that seem to spring from very different needs. For example, it could be assumed that people coming to a group for alcoholics have a common point of entry because they have a drinking problem.32 Superficially, the group may seem quite homogenous, insofar as everyone is there for drinking compulsively and to excess. However, clients may have turned to alcohol for significantly different reasons. Let's look at just one small group of three disparate individuals:

- Raul started drinking after he was passed over for promotion in favour of a friend: 'It was like being stabbed in the back.' His mother had died in the previous year.
- Lorenzo is in the habit of using alcohol to cope with his crippling shyness in social situations. His drunkenness recently saw him fired from his job as a security guard.
- Miriam has acknowledged that she resorts to drinking too much because she is angry with herself because she doesn't seem to be able to stay in a relationship. She woke up in ER having her stomach pumped recently, after a break-up with her last boyfriend and was badly frightened by how close she came to 'ending it all.'

Common behaviours

- Raul saw himself as abandoned and alone, and found the friend who never let him down in alcohol.

- Lorenzo uses alcohol as a crutch because he finds it very difficult to interact with others without something to make him feel braver and more sociable.
- Miriam experiences her life as a constant battle, dealing with her anger for herself, and her fear of others. Alcohol is the only thing that seems reliable, and it also seems to calm her nerves.

Common treatment expectation versus diverse perceptions of treatment goals

- Raul needs to stop drinking altogether. He is beginning to recognise serious consequences to his health and the quality of his work.
- Lorenzo does not consider himself an alcoholic and hopes to learn how to drink in a more controlled manner.
- Miriam does not hope or expect to stop drinking, but feels that she has a great need for emotional support with the anger and negative emotions that she associates with her situation and behaviour.

Standardised and individualised therapist treatment goals

In such a group, there is clearly common ground insofar as everyone has acknowledged an association between their drinking and their other problems. However, a challenge facing the facilitator is now how to isolate individual needs and figure out how to meet them.

- Raul, who has problems surrounding issues of competency and respect has an enlarged liver and is afraid of getting ill. He must learn how to cope with solitude without alcohol and needs to learn the skills necessary for developing a positive social circle. Group therapy will offer him the opportunity to acquire these skills.
- Lorenzo, who also has problems surrounding respect and competency, is concerned about his degree of control '(power') over his alcohol intake. The root of the problem lies with the anxiety he feels in social situations. Group therapy offers him a chance to learn how to interact with others, and acquire the self-control he needs to limit his own drinking.
- Miriam, whose dysfunctional behaviours spring from loyalty and abandonment issues, is the most difficult member of the group to approach. She is unable to verbalise her own needs, and presents with a compound of problems, including internalised anger, inappropriate self-medication

and depression. She seems to be in a 'vicious circle' because she will not be able to fully engage in therapy without stopping drinking and she feels that she cannot stop drinking until she feels better. Ideally, she will be able to come to view the group as her first safe relationship, a place where she can experiment with the emotional risk-taking required to accept her pain without numbing out.

Any group, regardless of whether its members have all come to therapy with the 'same' stated reason, may contain a wide variety of problem and goal definitions, socio-economic and educational backgrounds, family and/or medical histories, strengths of motivation, social and verbal skills, in addition to each client's original point of entry. In view of the many differences that exist in apparently homogeneous groups – insofar as all the clients are presenting with the same or similar maladaptive behaviours – it is important for the therapist to use universal therapeutic concepts that can be adapted to each client's unique requirements.

The themes and emotions behind these needs will generally correspond to the client's unmet relational needs – our universal themes, as listed above. By being identified as themes that everyone can relate to, the problem becomes something that can be discussed by the whole group. As the unmet needs emerge in the context of the therapy, they will be described and discussed with a vocabulary that everyone can understand and relate to, even if their own unmet needs are very different to those of all others in the therapeutic unit.

Addressing unmet needs in group context

Emerging theme

In this scenario, client issues are addressed as soon as they arise within the context of the group. The client-paced model develops each session's agenda according to the various themes that emerge in the group's discussion, by identifying these, expressing them in words and phrases that can be readily understood, and highlighting how these themes are relevant to the clients' emotional experience and the unmet needs that lie behind the behaviour that has brought them to therapy. This process ensures that clients are being heard, and that their needs become the centre of importance within group treatment[33]. The role of the therapist must be to listen very carefully to the individual clients' statements and unite them as a theme that will address the group's mandate, whatever that may be; in the case discussed above in some detail, the group's mandate is to focus on alcohol abuse. By focusing on emerging themes, even if the group is following a curriculum (see below), the therapist can work with the clients in the 'here and now' by addressing topics that are currently of concern.

Avoiding being driven by a curriculum

Many organisations offering therapeutic services feel a need to present curricula in order to demonstrate to the wider world that they are covering certain topics and that all prescribed topics will be covered within a discrete period of time. Clearly, closed groups are more likely to be presented as following a certain curriculum than open groups, which are perforce adaptable in their approach. Even in more flexible open groups, however, agencies offering therapy may feel compelled to 'cover' certain material, in order to rationalise their services. The danger therefore exists that a lack of flexibility will develop, to the detriment of the group members.

Inexperienced or improperly trained group workers may feel under pressure to 'stick' with an agenda rigidly, regardless of their clients' needs and the dynamic of the group. For example, if a group member discusses the lack of support he perceives from his colleagues at work and asks for help in addressing this situation, he could be told by a curriculum driven therapist that this will just have to wait until week five, when 'problem solving' is going to be discussed! While clearly certain issues need to be covered in any given therapeutic unit, rigidly conforming to a timetable is inappropriate in the extreme. One must always remember that a therapy group is a social unit, and that interaction in a social context is invariably 'circular' rather than following the format of one thing after another. Flexibility is key and the promotion of an emerging theme discussion, within the context of the curriculum topic at hand, is paramount.

Tools that can help

The Needs ABC model has a firm mandate – to help clients achieve psychological wellness and the ability to productively negotiate the challenges of their everyday lives – but in the therapeutic context, it is always client focussed. The therapist encourages dialogue around the issue introduced into the group by the clients, and draws this dialogue towards the theme-based emotions that are at the root of the unmet needs that are being described.

A variety of tools or props can help the therapist assist clients in 'tuning in to' the universal themes that they are experiencing. These can help by focussing attention on the salient emotional issues that the therapist feels underlie the topic at hand while, conversely, defocusing attention from the dysfunctional behaviours themselves and onto the unmet needs that lie behind the behaviours. The most commonly used tools are worth mentioning briefly:

Feelings chart

One such is the 'feelings chart' – a piece of paper that lists a wide range of emotions categorised in ordinary language. This tool provides clients with the vocabulary they need to express emotions that they might be resisting or ignoring and makes it easier for them to identify themselves with emotions that they may find awkward and embarrassing. This vocabulary is provided in the form of schematic drawings of universally interpretable grimaces and body language. Especially in the early stages of therapy, vocalising feelings of fear or anxiety or whatever the client has been struggling with can be difficult. Pointing to an image and then reading its label facilitates the communication of the emotion without the need for isolating and vocalising an unwelcome term. Feelings charts portray emotions schematically and in a manner that is much less equivocal than words. Understanding body language and facial expressions is instinctive and understood at 'gut' level, while mere words can be cloaked in ambiguity. Using a chart like that depicted below34 is sometimes called 'reaching for feelings.'

Role play

Role play is the term used to describe a scenario in which members of group 'take on' another person's character and situation in order to act out how they imagine that person would respond to a given situation. Clearly, this is a tool that is useful in all types of therapies, including group work. By stepping 'into someone else's shoes,' the client acquires a degree of objectivity from their own situation and is released from the restrictions their own unmet needs and maladaptive behaviours place on them. Role play (as we will discuss in more detail in the relevant sections below) can also be used in family or couple work, with clients asked to imagine themselves in the position of spouse, parents, children or siblings, so as to acquire some insight into how and why these people react to the situation under discussion. In a group work setting, there are more perspectives on how to handle a given situation than in individual, couple or family work, but role-plays always give the client an opportunity to practice appropriate discussions of unmet needs and enforce the concept of collaborative problem-solving. At the same time, many people find it easier to voice potentially awkward observations when they are out of character and are, in fact, pretending to be somebody else. The therapist's role should be to know when to sit back and 'keep out of it' but also to know when to intervene so as to keep the role play on track and away from destructive interactions between clients. For example, if a group member has a particular need that is not being met in her relationship, the group members can 'couple up' and demonstrate how they might resolve this issue if it applied to them. The distressed client can then practice a demonstrated approach or draw from the various examples given and integrate a strategy that would be most comfortable for her to attempt.

Time-out, logging and business meetings

Other tools that can be used both in the context of therapy and in the wider world, helping clients to identify their unmet needs and express them succinctly in terms of the universal themes outlined above include 'time out,' 'logging' and 'business meetings.'

'Time out' provides clients with a concrete technique that gives them a mechanism that they can use to break their dysfunctional behavioural patterns, to help those whom they care about feel safe with them and to give them the time they need to identify a viable alternative to the behaviours they have used to date. Clients are taught that they need to discuss this tool with important people in their lives so that they can instigate it as a new element of their behaviour. This technique consists of simply leaving the scene of stress and triggers to inappropriate behaviour and taking some time to calm down, acquire some perspective and arrive at a new approach for re-entering the potentially stressful situation.

'Logging' is just what it sounds like. Clients are encouraged to note down the circumstances of times when they feel that they may start to display the dysfunctional behaviour that has brought them to therapy. A table can be provided to assist with this task, as below:

A 'business meeting' follows the client's time out and self-examination. Having determined what the trigger to the dysfunctional behaviour was, how he was feeling and why, he asks the individual or group implicit in the situation to meet with him to discuss his findings in a calm, level-headed way, without casting guilt or aspersions. For example, a client who has fears associated with abandonment or loyalty issues might feel badly when her partner promises to help her with something in the house but does not show as promised. She could tell her partner: 'I was pretty upset the other day when you did not show. I was feeling alone and abandoned, much like I did when my parents didn't pick me up at school when they promised to do so.' Here the client recognises that the feelings are her problems but is also reminding her partner that reliability is important to her because of her unfortunate life experiences from the past. As well, this helps her partner to be more objective about her statement to him by understanding that he is not primary to her experience of loyalty or abandonment.

Recognising the emotional component of the universal theme

While therapy and the effective use of tools such as those outlined above can help clients identify when and why they display dysfunctional behaviours, a key to moving beyond their problems lies in recognising the emotions behind the themes that emerge from their self-examination and in the context of therapy. Let's look at some examples.

The following are statements made by the three clients whom we have already met in the context of their alcohol abuse treatment group, Raul, Lorenzo and Miriam. Even though they have the same behavioural problem, they have different theme-based issues producing different emotions.

> Raul: 'Drinking relaxes me especially at parties. I don't know why, but when I don't drink I always feel that I am going to make a mess of it. After I throw back a couple I feel more like a world-beater.' Here Raul is able to identify his problem with drinking as relating to his need to feel that he can engage with others in an open way without the fear of ridicule.

In other words, he has issues surrounding competency. He drinks too much because it seems to give him the social confidence he lacks – he is afraid – a problem that originated in childhood from parents who were both unsupportive and critical.

Lorenzo: 'I have the opposite problem. I often feel that others don't care about what I say. At the last party I was at I actually saw somebody stifle a yawn as I was talking.' Lorenzo grew up as an only child of older parents who were very preoccupied with their own life issues and never seemed to have time to devote to him, frequently leaving him for days on end with his elderly grandmother who was, of necessity, somewhat removed from him because she was profoundly deaf. Lorenzo's problems are centred around respect. As a child, Lorenzo found comfort in the candies his grandmother gave him to eat – they helped him to deal with his profound sadness; in adulthood similar 'comfort' of a sort has been found in alcohol.

Miriam: I feel a little like both of you. I try to say as little as possible or make uninteresting small talk because I am afraid that, if I say anything important, someone will eventually use it against me.' Miriam grew up in a profoundly dysfunctional family. Her father was a violent man who beat his wife, causing both wife and daughter to feel betrayed by the man who should have cared for them both. Miriam's mother was a routine abuser of prescription drugs. Although both parents loved their daughter, they also used her as a pawn in their own domestic disputes. Understandably, Miriam has experienced a lot of unresolved anger about this.

In therapy, Raul, Lorenzo and Miriam learn how to express their unique situations with the help of the therapist, who 'links' what they say to the universal themes, and assists them in understanding the emotions behind these themes. Focusing on universal themes helps clients to discover the needs that are underlying their maladaptive behaviours and where they originate, and this is a crucial breakthrough on the journey to emotional wellness. Clearly, however, recognising these behaviours is not enough. It is also necessary to understand the appropriate – more useful – emotional component that provokes this behaviour in order to devise new strategies for dealing with unmet needs.

6
The uncovered needs-deficit and what to do with it

The beauty of the Needs ABC Model lies largely in the fact that it focuses on universals, rather than specifics; on the emotions and needs that we all experience rather than the particular, unique ways in which each of us deals with them. This 'universal' view enables diverse people to work together, and to understand that, regardless of how different their situation may seem and feel to others, at base we are all searching for much the same things and seek the emotional fulfilment we all require from our relationships with other people. It should be understood that the purpose of the Needs ABC model is not to suggest that everyone is 'the same' or that identical approaches will work for everyone, but rather that we all have much more in common that might initially appear to be the case.

The Needs ABC has developed a technique for identifying and investigating the above-mentioned client relational needs by using the nine universal themes developed by Caplan and Thomas, as outlined in the previous chapter. These universal themes refer to basic needs or emotional obstacles that are experienced by us all at one time or another and that can become impediments to healthy behavioural habits when they seem to be unable to meet. Generally, the client's expression of these unmet needs is not overtly described by him, but is, instead, embedded in his descriptions of life situations that are traumatic or stressful. Rather than searching for direct references to the key emotions behind problematic behaviours, the therapist should learn the 'language' of unmet needs and become equipped to identify and vocalise the relevant theme and emotion in each instance.

Isolating universal themes

Let's look at ways in which the universal themes are typically expressed in a therapeutic environment, and ways in which the therapist can 'tap in' to the themes so as to facilitate deeper exploration:

Abandonment[35]

For example, in a group for children from divorced families, one client said: *'My father said he was going to pick me up after school today and take me to the group. He never made it.'*

The therapist then suggested: *'It must be very sad to think that just when you think you're getting closer, he leaves you again.'*

Betrayal

A fifty-year-old business man in a substance abuse treatment facility said: *'I miss my son so much and yesterday was the last straw. He told me that, even though I was finally getting help, he was not going to visit me until he was sure I was serious.'*

The counsellor then proposed to the group: *'I guess a lot of you can relate to how sad it is when others let you down.'*

Intimacy

Simon, in a relationship problems group, stated: *'My week has been pretty good except for one small problem ... my wife seems to be avoiding me. She's never home when I am. Either I'm looking after the kids or she is ... we're* never together. She's even too busy to go out for dinner – the two of us.'

The group facilitator replied: 'It must be sad to think that she doesn't want to get closer to you.'

Respect

Client in an outpatient recovery group: 'Last night I was in bed sound asleep and at two in the morning my best friend in L.A. called – scared the heck out of me! He knows what time it is on the West Coast. What's up with him?!'

Therapist (to the group): 'It seems lousy to realise how difficult it is to gain back respect from others.'

Competence

Client (in a single parent support group): 'My ex-wife just kills me! I told her that I would help her wallpaper the kids' bedroom. First we select wallpaper together, then I spend the weekend putting it up, and then she tells me she doesn't like it anymore. I guess I just can't do anything right.'

Group facilitator: 'It's sad to think that Jon still can't get it right'

Responsibility

For example, Jordie, attending a domestic violence treatment group, told his peers that *he couldn't change since his wife was always 'egging him on.'*

The worker replied: 'It seems to me that it is scary for Jordie to look at his responsibility in all of this.'

Power

Joanne, attending a women's support group, stated: 'I'm getting a little fed up. Every time I come home from work my boyfriend is in a bad mood. He's had a lousy day at work or he's got a headache or the car is not working properly. I've tried to explain my position in every conceivable way. He just doesn't get it. There's nothing more I can do!'

To this, the group worker responded: 'Gosh ... It must be frustrating to feel so powerless in a relationship.'

Grief/loss

A woman in a gambler's addiction treatment group angrily explained: 'I've lost my job, my husband, my family. I don't have any credit anywhere. Before I started to gamble life was great; now it sucks. I don't care; nothing matters anymore.'

A group member replied: 'I know it's annoying to face the truth, but once you accept it you will move on.'

By focusing on the emotionally laden universal themes embedded in the clients' words rather than on the specific content of them, the facilitator is able to go beyond simple complaints to promote a theme-based discussion of relational needs rather than content-oriented quick solutions or 'game plans.' This also has the benefit of opening discussion to the group, and of making it possible to propose solutions that may be useful for more than one group member to consider. The key to solving the issue of the problematic behaviours that have brought the client to therapy will not be found by addressing the behaviours head on, but by finding out what unmet needs lie behind them and devising new, unproblematic ways in which these needs can be met. Similarly, by referring to the universal themes in a non-directive way, the therapist avoids risking appearing judgemental, and facilitates other members of the group or therapeutic unit in identifying with the topic at hand.

The technique of uncovering the relevant theme in a client's narrative can help them understand what is lacking in their important relationships (needs deficits), and help the group facilitator to link clients, promote a common purpose, objectively validate different viewpoints and bring apparently peripheral participants into the group process. A universal theme focus also promotes collaboration in the group by defining issues more globally so that more group members can readily participate in discussing and working towards a solution of each others' situations. Thus, towards violence, the group looks at the unmet needs that prompt John and Marcia to engage in destructive behaviours, and alternative ways in which they can try to meet these needs.

Let's look at how this approach can work in practice by exploring a case study:

From the specific to the general

In the example below, taken from a group therapy session, one woman's frustration with her father's forgetfulness can be related to universal feelings of 'respect,' 'betrayal,' or 'abandonment.' Although other members of the group have not experienced the same specific problem, they are all able to relate to the universal feelings embedded in her narrative:

Example: Julie

Julie was a thirty-five year old mother of three who married Trevor, her 'childhood sweetheart,' right after she graduated from high school. She had been going out with Trevor since the age of fourteen and decided to 'go all the way' at the age of seventeen when she was in her last year of high school. She and Trevor had enrolled in separate colleges, each some distance away from their home town, and it was not clear if they would be able to remain together. At the time, Julie felt that she was offering Trevor 'a gift.'

Shortly after graduation, Julie was dismayed to discover that she had become pregnant, since she had originally wanted to go to law school. Despite some misgivings, she decided to keep the child with a promise from Trevor that he would do his utmost to support her financially as well as share in the parenting. Julie's parents had been against her keeping the child and had told her emphatically that: *'If you decide to keep the child you will have to take care of it!'*

Though disappointed that she would have to put her education on hold, Julie took her parents' words as a challenge. They had never been that supportive and had divorced around the time that she began to date Trevor. In the meantime, Trevor seemed to work longer hours and become less involved with both Julie and their infant. Because the young couple did not have much financial support from their parents, Trevor had also had to forgo college and instead worked in a series of blue-collar jobs that he felt were beneath his dignity as someone who had graduated high school with grades high enough to attend 'any college he wanted.'

Julie convinced Trevor to have another child and gave birth to their second just after their first child turned two. Julie always had always wanted a 'large family' (she was an only child) and she felt that taking care of two would be as easy as caring for one, and that as she had decided to be a mother, she might as well 'do it properly.'

In the meantime, Trevor became less and less available, using the financial commitment of providing for his family as an excuse, and when Julie became pregnant with their third, against her husband's wishes, Trevor admitted to being unfaithful with one of his co-workers and asked for a divorce.

Julie was devastated. She had been so busy with her children that she had lost all contact with her friends. Her mother had moved to Europe and remarried, and her father had never been reliable because of his drinking and partying – especially since his wife had left. Julie also began to drink and it was only a matter of time before child protection services were called in and she was given an ultimatum to get help for her drinking or lose custody of her children. Julie sought help at a government funded substance abuse treatment facility close to her home town, in their outpatient department, so she could continue to be with her children while dealing with her substance abuse problem.

Since Trevor continued to distance himself from his role as 'father' and to remain absent from his children's lives, Julie tried to enlist her father for some emotional and practical support. In fact, Julie's dad had been able to baby-sit on several occasions without incident. However, there were also several occasions when he was unavailable because of his drinking.

During one of Julie's group therapy sign-ins she recounted her devastation at her father, once again, letting her down.

Averting her eyes from the gaze of her fellow group members, Julie began to talk:

'My father said he was going to go shopping with me yesterday but called at the last minute to tell me he was having 'just one more drink with the

boys.' He never made it. I have decided that I don't have a father anymore.' As she finished speaking, her voice began to break but she bit her lip so as to avoid crying.

On hearing the story, other members of the group begin to chime in that Julie's father is 'no good' and that she is 'better off without him.'

Far from being reassuring, these comments seemed to make Julie feel worse. She sank into a morose silence and contemplated her feet on the carpet, apparently reluctant to say any more or to engage further with the other members of the group.

On listening to Julie's story, and knowing something of her background, the therapist could rely on the following schematic to formulate a process oriented intervention for the group:

The therapist listens to Julie's story and tries to think about how she is feeling about what is being said. In this case, the therapist's initial reaction concurs with that of the other group members, that the Julie's father is extremely selfish in choosing his friends over his daughter.

The therapist then thinks about what Julie actually wants (client need) or does not yet have (needs-deficit).

For example, the show of frustration could be an attempt to bring her father closer ('If you loved me...'). Or,

The statement might also represent Julie's frustration with other important relationships in her life.

The therapist constructs a hypothesis about the Julie's theme-based process.

Julie is afraid of completely losing her father, emotionally and concretely. Or,

Julie perceives herself as being unimportant in the world.

The therapist formulates a theme-based, emotion-focused, statement reflecting the process in Julie's story, taking into consideration her stage of development in the group. There are least three possibilities for what Julie is missing in her relationship(s): feeling important, needing emotional reliability, or both. The therapist knows that these unmet needs of respect or abandonment are common and that once they are identified, most of the other group members will recognise when they have also had these feelings in relationships and whether they have been able to successfully deal with them. This will make it possible for them to offer real, constructive advice to Julie, based on their own experiences. The above schematic can be used to formulate the following theme-based, emotion-focused, intervention, based on the universal themes of respect or abandonment.

Theme-based statement (made as an observation to the group):

'It seems that Julie is pretty upset that her father values his friends more than his daughter.'

Comments

Because clients often relate their emotional states to others inadequately, understanding the underlying, more productive, emotion embedded in a narrative is used to help each group work participant understand their emotional needs in relationships more clearly. A productive emotion is one that is more 'useful' in problem resolution, potentially leading to a better outcome at the time of the relational interchange. In other words, a productive emotion is one that predicts a better resolution to the problem at hand at the time of the relational interchange. For example, a man's expression of 'fear' or 'sadness' should cause a less defensive reaction in his partner than if he expresses his relational concerns from a position of anger. A 'secondary,'[36] less productive, emotion (like 'anger' in the previous example) is often presented because it is more culturally acceptable in the situation at hand and therefore more easily expressed although it may, in effect, worsen the predicament. When Julie tearfully describes her father's disloyalty, she may well be sad (the less productive emotion) but is also most probably angry (the more workable 'primary' emotion)[37]. Whereas sadness and despair may be immobilising, anger can be motivating. If Julie can recognise her resentment, she will be more likely to motivate herself to become more assertive with her father and, ultimately, in other relationships. Adding the more appropriate emotional component to the interpretation of process, the therapist can formulate a statement reflecting a more productive emotional component of the process in the client's story, taking into consideration the client's stage of development in the group, as follows:

- Suggested less productive emotion: 'sadness.'
- Suggested more productive emotion: 'anger.'

The therapist constructs a more specifically emotion focused process statement, and makes it to the group as a whole, saying:

Fig. 8. Feeling faces

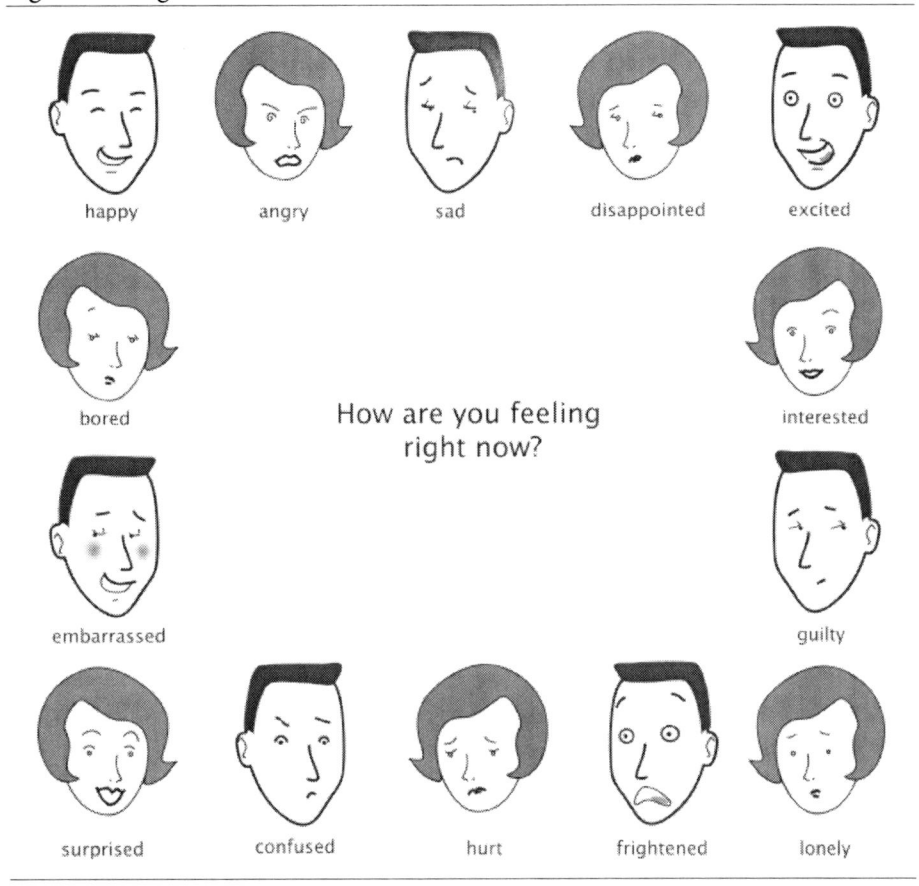

happy	angry	sad	disappointed	excited
bored		How are you feeling right now?		interested
embarrassed				guilty
surprised	confused	hurt	frightened	lonely

'It seems that Julie is really angry that her father values his friends more than his daughter.'

Using this combination of techniques, facilitators can also guide the group toward productive relational problem-solving strategies. For example, the facilitator and the group collaborate on the following action plan through a group 'survey' or role-play:

- With the use of a feelings chart (see Fig. 8, above), ask each member to distinguish between the presenting emotion and the more empowering emotion in Julie's narrative.
- From a list of universal themes, ask each member to suggest what they feel is Julie's unmet need.
- Problem-solve, or role-play, possibilities for the expression of the more useful emotion in ways that will functionally describe the unmet need.

When using the above intervention map, it is important to identify and ally with the client's expressed emotions while supportively challenging ineffective behaviours. The following dynamic helps to explain the significance of the above:

- The needs deficit (theme) drives emotions.
- Emotions drive behaviours.
- Presenting, less useful, emotions tend to drive problematic behaviours.
- More useful emotions tend to validate the client's experience and offer more appropriate options for satisfying unmet needs.
- Problem-solving through collaborative work encourages more options for functional approaches to getting needs met.
- When needs are met appropriately, problematic behaviours are extinguished.
- Uncomfortable emotions will always exist, but problematic ways of coping with unmet needs will gradually be discontinued.

There are several advantages to interpreting the emotional possibilities along with client process theme by means of the universal themes present in the client's narrative. Because the narrative content is seldom universal but the process theme usually is, an effective emotion-focused intervention touches on situations that all members can relate to. Because those who enter a group setting are often anxious about being confronted, exposed, or punished, connecting with the client in a meaningful, reassuring way can be a delicate procedure. In the case cited above, focusing on universally experienced theme, and the embedded felt emotions, makes it possible for Julie, the other group members, and the facilitator to connect in a way that just would not have been possible if they had remained focused on the specifics of Julie's story. The true issue at hand was not that Julie's father had stood her up, or even that Julie is finding it hard to control her drinking, but that her drinking has developed as a result of her anger at finding herself in a situation where she does not feel acknowledged or, indeed, valuable. If Julie can learn how to use her anger more productively, rather than try to hide it, she will no longer experience the need to drink to excess.

Now, let's turn to another example, in this case involving a man with violence issues that he urgently needs to resolve:

Example: Jorge

Jorge, a thirty-five-year-old Canadian of Spanish descent, had been both verbally and physically violent to his wife, often in the presence of his eight-year-old twin daughters, Candida and Olivia. Jorge also had an eighteen-month-old son, the son he had always wanted (in fact, for much of his daughters' lives, Jorge had lamented that neither had been born of the 'right' sex: *'There's nobody to carry on the family name!'*)

Because of Jorge's physical and verbal violence, his wife Violetta finally asked him to leave after an incident when he hit her, broke several of the windows in the house and reduced the little girls to tears.

Before attending group therapy, Jorge has a screening interview with the group facilitator, who affirms Jorge's apparent willingness to engage in therapy, while making it clear that his violent abuse of his wife is in no way acceptable, and that the primary goal of therapy must be the complete elimination of such behaviour. During sign-in, at the first session, Jorge is asked to introduce himself, and to accept his ownership of his behaviour. As Jorge's participation in group therapy continues, the other group members, and the therapist, gradually learn more about him:

As a child, Jorge had come to Canada with his mother, whom he had never felt to be supportive or encouraging. (*'No matter how hard I tried, she always compared me unfavourably to someone else.'*) It had been with relief that he had moved out on graduating from high school and finding a job. Yet, years later, when Jorge's wife asked him to leave, he moved back in with his mother. Jorge's cultural background, in which women very much rule the roost in the domestic domain and men are not supposed to engage in domestic tasks, may be partly behind this decision, but this does not completely explain Jorge's feeling that he cannot or should not live on his own. He offered by way of excuse that he cannot cook and cannot afford rent and child support, and that it will be easier for him to get by if his mother helps out: *'So now I'm supposed to keep house as well as bring home the bacon? I don't think so!'*

Jorge continued to be aggressive with his wife in the presence of his daughters on the few occasions that Violetta allowed him to spend time with them. Finally, Violetta obtained a divorce and a restraining order that allowed him visitation with his children only if he received treatment for his violence. Jorge had previously engaged in three courses of treatment at other violence clinics, completing only the third. The restraining order was terminated; but his abusive behaviours resurfaced.

This time, Jorge seems to have returned to treatment willingly, acknowledging that he has reached the critical point where something had to change.

'I know I have to change,' Jorge said the first time he attended the group. *'I've been in groups before, but I realise that I have yet to change my attitude and that I didn't get very far. This time I want to learn how to do better and to take charge of my own behaviour, like you said [indicating therapist].'*

After having been quite quiet throughout much of the meeting, Jorge later remarked: 'I'm also really depressed. I know I'm completely responsible for what's happened. I love my wife and children with all my heart, and all I can think about is when we will all be together as a family again. My father left my mother when I was a kid so I know how hard it is to grow up without a dad and my mother has basically humiliated me for my whole freakin' life. Sometimes I think she hates me because I look like my father. My wife smokes, and Candida and Olivia have asthma. When I tell her that she shouldn't smoke in the house, she tells me to 'f__k off' because smoking is the one pleasure she has left and threatens that she won't ever let me see my children again if I give her a hard time. She told me that she knows I don't care about the twins because they are girls, but that's not true. I love them just as much as my son, even if I find them harder to relate to. This group is my last resort. If I can't get help here I don't know what I'm going to do.'

Jorge seems to sincerely be ready to change, but it is not hard to see that the prospect is also frightening for him and that he is feeling thoroughly overwhelmed by his situation. Jorge is afraid that he will have to change not just his behaviours but also what he sees as his ingrained personality. To explore areas of defensiveness, we can imagine what is going Jorge's mind, bearing in mind that such internal monologues often occur below the level of conscious thought and tend to be complex and multi-faceted.

In his statements to the group, Jorge may be 'testing' his fellow members and the facilitator to confirm his worst fears about himself, the world, and therapy. He certainly seems to view the world as a series of negative events and to suspect that he is doomed to follow a trajectory that has already been mapped out. Beneath his conscious level of thought, Jorge's inner monologue might sound something like this:

'I'm afraid of saying the wrong thing. I don't want to be punished. I've

already been punished and humiliated enough. What I really want is for you to confirm that I'm not a sick person and to acknowledge that I'm not physically violent any more. What if I can't hold my family together by coming to therapy? O.K., I accept that I'm responsible for hitting Violetta, but I don't see why I should go on being punished. It sucks finding myself back at Mom's at my age, without being able to see my kids. I don't like having to put up with being bossed around by my mother as if I was a little kid. I understand that it's not right to hit women, but losing my family is out of line. What if, despite all the changes I make, Violetta can't see how far I've come? No matter what I do, she doesn't trust me. If she can't see me trying, why should I try?'

Comment

How social interactions take place in therapy has a big impact on the way client and therapist alike respond to the therapeutic environment. It is crucial, for example, for clients to feel involved and included in their own process of change, rather than 'put upon.' It is important that they be allowed to speak and take charge of their own dysfunctional behaviours and approaches to dealing with them.

In the case above, Jorge's progress might be negatively affected if he sees the group as an extension of all of the authority figures who have 'bossed him around' in his life, especially his mother. This might lead to his viewing the group as punitive, and considering it as an integral part of his current unsatisfactory situation, in which he is living with his mother and is not always free to do whatever he wants. By displaying defensiveness, Jorge might seek on some level for permission to leave the group in an attempt to gain some mastery over his own life.

To help Jorge view the group as a positive place rather than a punishment, he will need to feel included, and he will need help in finding the 'voice' he currently lacks when he attempts to interact with his mother and his wife. His apparent reluctance to disclose details of his experience may be a way to ask to be 'fixed' without having to take responsibility for his own behaviour.

What can the facilitator do to penetrate the layers of anxiety that are preventing Jorge from a full and honest exploration of his emotional landscape? By avoiding a narrow focus on the specifics of Jorge's story – and thus avoiding displaying anger or disgust – the therapist can focus on the universal themes and emotions embedded in his narrative instead. This broader focus will remove the blame/guilt element from the situation and enable Jorge and the rest of the group to examine his problematic behaviours in a helpful way and come up with strategies he can use.

Several theme-based emotions are quite clear from Jorge's narrative:

- Whenever anything happens to make him feel abandoned or discounted, Jorge tends to respond with violence – the undesired, unacceptable behaviour;
- Jorge is afraid that his children will cease to love him;
- Jorge is afraid that his own life story will be recreated if his children lose him;
- Jorge's unresolved grief about his father's abandonment of his family when he was a child has resulted in feelings of anger towards his parents. This anger has been extended to his wife when she appears to be abandoning him, too. Now, Jorge feels that he is alone, that his wife, mother and the legal system have 'ganged up on' him and that he is punished while others escape scot-free. Jorge has developed the tendency to use violence and intimidation against Violetta in a useless attempt to get 'in charge' of his situation, but with exactly the opposite effect.

An emotion-focussed, theme-based, approach to Jorge's situation will allow the therapist to negotiate his own reaction to this difficult client by placing the attention firmly on the client's needs and generalising the emotional themes in his narrative to the group.

A framework of this process could be as follows:

1. *Still seeking help – not ready to give up*
   Need for support (marginalisation)
2. *Fear of lack of control in his life*
   Need for reassurance (competency)

3. *Fear that others will take advantage of him*
   Need for loyalty (betrayal)

4. *Desire to do things on his own terms*
   Need for safety and control (power)

By making Jorge's feelings accessible to the rest of the group, he will become involved in the group, and vice versa. By initially avoiding focussing on Jorge's unpleasant behaviours, the risk that he will be, as he sees it, attacked further, is minimised. Later, when he has begun to feel more comfortable in the group setting and understand how his less useful emotions have led to less productive problem-solving, interventions can be made to help group members to supportively challenge his problematic behaviours, and examine those which will better meet his relational needs. For example, referring to Jorge's multiple negative experiences of treatment, the therapist could offer support by saying:

> 'Even though it appears that, no matter what you try, it doesn't work out the way you expected, you are still not willing to throw in the towel and that means that, deep down, you know that you can change what needs to be changed.'

When Jorge explains how he felt powerless in the world around him as a child who was humiliated, abandoned, and deprived, the therapist might reassure him with this process statement:

> 'It must be frightening to see horrible things happening around you and feel that there is nothing you can do. I guess you're wondering if you have any control here.'

When Jorge uses the phrases, 'Learn from my mistakes,' and 'If I can't get help here, I don't know what I'll do,' he may be indicating his need to feel competent. He appears to feel that people exploit him and experiences himself as vulnerable. The therapist might acknowledge genuine feelings of apprehension in the following empathic way:

> 'Goodness, if I'd been through what Jorge's been through been through, I wouldn't know when to let my guard down.'

To Jorge's expressions of his inability to have a say in how his life should unfold, the therapist could offer:

> 'I guess Jorge is wondering how he's going to get his turn to be in control.'

Any one of the above interventions will make it possible for Jorge to 'let his guard down' and engage with the therapist and the group. These approaches maintain a focus on Jorge's unmet needs rather than his behaviours. This helps the facilitator to help Jorge get away from the 'blame game' and take a more useful approach towards solving the problem of his violent behaviours.

Effective theme-based statements illuminate a theme within the narrative that all group members can relate to. Who would not feel encouraged by statements that support, include and reassure?

Sustaining group process

Overall, it is important that the therapist uses statements that connect with an individual and help them to engage in therapy. Ultimately, however, it is group process that sustains an atmosphere of collaborative problem solving. Effective therapy is accomplished through the use of group process to elicit empathy as well as challenging interpretations from members. In group process, members of the group can relate to others' problems and solutions and use these insights to develop and adopt appropriate and useful coping skills. When this is achieved, individual clients will feel more validated, competent and connected to others.

Kurland and Salmon[38] have outlined the importance of differentiating group process from individual case work in a group. In the case of Jorge, the therapist has made a number of process statements that were inclusive of the entire group, encouraging group members to expand on the themes of 'power,' 'competency,' 'marginalization' and 'loyalty.' For example, the above example of validating Jorge's feelings of inadequacy could be proffered to the group as follows:

> 'It seems that we all have had the experience that, no matter what we try, it doesn't work out the way we expected, yet we still don't give up.'

This would allow for group members to disclose situations in which they have felt similarly and to dialogue around what strategies they had used to remain motivated to solve the problem.

Needs vs. behaviour

It cannot be said often enough that focusing on the specifics of a client's narrative rather than the theme-based emotions behind the 'story' can make it very difficult to intervene in a fruitful way. For example, if a man describes his wife's emotionally 'abusive' aloofness and independence and the facilitator thinks: 'That really sucks! I would be so angry if that happened to me,' she risks becoming an 'ally' of the client in light of his wife's behaviour and, by extension, of the maladaptive behaviours that have brought him to therapy. If, instead, the therapist understands that the man's anger was probably that he did not feel acknowledged – that he feels that he needs respect – or validated for his hard work and parenting and that this was scary for him – in light of the issues he has surrounding competency – the group can then examine some possibilities to help the man meet his relational needs.

Maintaining focus on a client's behaviour may reinforce the shame or misgivings that they already have about what brings them in for help. Most clients know on some level when their problem-solving strategies are inappropriate – after all, this has what brought them to therapy in the first place, whether they came voluntarily or not. The question they need to answer is, 'what matters so much that you will do almost anything to get it?'

When a relational need is not being met, it is important for the client to understand what is missing as clearly as possible in order to begin to consider new, more appropriate, strategies. When the need or needs that have been elusive are illuminated, the potential for avoidant behaviour in the therapeutic setting will appear to diminish. For example, when a client is confronted with the reality that he has been sent to treatment by his Employee Assistance Program for smelling of alcohol at work, he may move away from his own responsibility by discussing his perceived lack of support in the workplace, thus revealing his fears of abandonment, and how, even though he 'has a couple to relax' at lunchtime, he has never avoided any of his responsibilities or commitment to his employer. If the facilitator suggests that he feels disconnected or lonely at work because he perceives himself to be abandoned, he should be able to speak more freely about the reality that there might be other, more practical, ways of dealing with his feelings of disconnection and loneliness.

For example, let's take a look at Darren, a seventeen-year-old high school student who has been sent to counselling by his parents for skipping classes, not handing in assignments and 'maybe smoking dope.' Darren is going to attend group therapy, but his counsellor meets him for a lengthy intake session, and decides that it would be useful to meet with him individually a few times before he enters the group. The first of three one-on-one sessions goes like this:

Counsellor: 'So, Darren, what is your impression of why you have to be here today?'

Darren: 'My folks make a big deal out of everything. They are perfection freaks.'

Counsellor: 'Would you mind giving me some examples?'

Darren: 'Well, first of all they think I am a drug addict. All my friends smoke a little 'weed' on the weekends. My friend Steve should be here – he smokes every day and he's still an honour student!'

Counsellor: *'Is that it?'*

Darren: *'I suppose they told you that I cut class last week. I didn't have my assignment done and, as soon as I finished it, I showed up to hand it in. I got a pretty good grade and I haven't missed one since. I really don't see what the problem is.'*

Counsellor: *'It seems to me that you are under a lot of pressure.'*

Darren: *'Yeah, my older sister is a whiz – she is applying to medical school. My father wants me to go into business but I just want to play my guitar. Natasha's like an angel and I'm supposed to be the black sheep of the family!'*

Counsellor: *'So you want to be a musician?'*

Darren: *'Well, I'm not really sure. Business is O.K. too I guess ... but I suck in math.*

Counsellor: *'What things are you good at?'*

Darren: *'Well ... I suppose I'm pretty good in English. I really love computers ... I set up this program so I can play along with a rhythm section...I am trying to add more instruments.'*

Counsellor: *'Do you want music to be a career?'*

Darren: *'Not really ... just a hobby.'*

Counsellor: *'So what would you like to do as a career?'*

Darren: *'The fact is I really don't know. My father keeps pushing me into business, and he's having some business problems of his own. I don't want to piss him off and give him more grief ... He still gives me an allowance even though we're tight. I mean, I suppose we have our problems but he's a nice guy.'*

The counsellor then went on to talk with Darren about his need to make his parents proud of him, having picked up on Darren's underlying need to be recognised as competent, and his fears that if he did not do what they asked of him, even if he would be unhappy doing it, that they would become angry, revealing his fears associated with the issue of abandonment. The counsellor then said:

'You know, Darren, I know that whatever you do you want to be good at and enjoy. It must be scary to think that if you let down your parents they will never forgive you.'

Darren lowered his head and said nothing. After a few seconds the counsellor said:

> 'Well, maybe there's a way to please your parents and please yourself. Maybe we should brainstorm together some possibilities that we could discuss with your parents – when you are ready – things that might be just as good as going into business. Things that would show them that you want to make them proud of you and that you would enjoy doing.'

At this point Darren became more engaged and, together with the counsellor, examined some appropriate vocational possibilities – including a summer job – that might be available in one of his areas of interest.

If the counsellor had focussed on any of Darren's behaviours by enquiring, for example, as to whether he has considered the consequences of them, it is probable that an adversarial position would have been established as opposed to a collaborative one. For instance, if the counsellor had focussed on Darren's use of marijuana and said:

> 'What if you had been found with marijuana in your possession? It's illegal. You could have gotten into trouble. And research shows that it smoking it can lead to short term memory loss! I guess you really didn't think, huh?'

Darren would have thought:

> 'I know what I did was silly. He's just like all the others, telling me what to do and what not to do. This jerk is treating me like a baby! Doesn't he realise I'm practically an adult? I'm leaving high school soon, but everywhere I go, people punish me for screwing up. I'm not coming back here!'

On the other hand, by keeping the focus on Darren's need to feel adequate in his endeavours, as well as to feel loved unconditionally, the therapist can be perceived as an ally. Then, once an alliance has been created, by looking together at the uncomfortable feelings that arise when Darren's needs seem unattainable, and what he does to try and alleviate this emotional discomfort, they can begin to examine more functional strategies Darren can use to work towards getting his needs met. In this case, meetings were later set up with the parents, individually and together, to improve communication around all of their relational needs.

The above demonstrates how focussing on needs versus behaviour will tend to lower client reluctance to collaborate on problem-solving. Although Darren made some progress individually, the counsellor felt that he would also benefit from some time in group therapy, suggesting:

> 'Maybe you can brainstorm together with others in the group some possibilities that you could discuss with your parents. I'm sure that you and the other group members will be able to work together towards some solutions to the issues that are bugging you.'

In the context of group therapy, it will be useful for Darren to continue to examine more appropriate ways of getting his needs met. Darren will be able to try out the strategies that emerge and report back to the group to continue the 'brainstorming' if needs be. Using these more functional strategies should Darren him to understand which needs he can acquire in his family relationships, and how to pursue them. Acquiring his relational needs should help Darren feel less emotionally anxious and less inclined to use less productive strategies in this relationship.

Universal themes and development

The Needs ABC model is helpful to clients as it moves them away from what they have done 'wrong' to what they can do to make things 'right.' It gives them an understanding of what they have been looking for in their relationships and examines the strategies that they have been using to get their needs met.

By focusing on the universal and not the particular, clients can be helped to identify productive alternatives to maladaptive behaviours, without becoming bogged down in their own personal fears and anxieties. To enable the Needs ABC model to work throughout the duration of therapy, the therapist must also maintain focus on barriers that can exist between the various people involved – barriers present from the outset and those that might develop within the therapeutic context – so that these can be dealt with and removed from the situation at hand.

The Needs ABC model postulates that most needs-getting strategies are formed predominantly in the earlier stages of development, from the preschool years through to adolescence, as we discussed earlier. As children, we are truly impotent captives of our environment, lacking the autonomy to make conscious choices with regard to problem-solving. It is during this period that we develop 'survival skills;' strategies that help us to deal with those uncomfortable feelings that arise when our needs are not being met. We often bring these strategies into adulthood when all else fails. It should be noted that what we experienced as children that made us feel good we continue to want as adults and what was missing for us as children that made us feel poorly is also sought in our adult years. We try to remain in relationships with others who seem to meet our needs. When we perceive that these needs are no longer being met, we attempt to reacquire them, and the more important they seem to us, the more effort is put into getting them. If nothing we do as an adult seems to be successful we often resort to strategies that are similar to those we used as children with some success. Additionally, where gender specific needs exist the theme would be acted out quite powerfully in the context of the couple's relationship.

Because most behavioural problems occur in a social context – the family, work, marriage, social and work relationships – it is essential to enable those presenting for therapy to become enabled to overcome the barriers that exist between them and the important people in their lives.

We now can turn our attention to how to eliminate those barriers using the Needs ABC Model in particular.

7
Eliminating barriers

AS GROUP MEMBERS, couples, families or individuals attend therapy over a period of time, it is important to foster and help to grow feelings of unity among the members or between the family members of the couple while at the same time 'nipping in the bud' unhealthy dynamics that may arise between the various members, or between certain members and the therapist.

To illustrate this, let's return to Darren, whose situation we looked at in the previous chapter. We will assume that Darren has been encouraged to attend group therapy following a period of individual therapy. As we already know, for Darren, a dominant theme is his need to feel adequate – his issues with competency – and a fear that he will be abandoned if 'does not measure up.' The way he has handled not getting this need in the past was by getting into trouble at school to deflect attention from his mediocre academic performance and generally giving his parents cause for concern. This behaviour has been successful for Darren in preventing him from being criticised about his felt inadequacy in meeting the expectations of others, both at home and at school, albeit with negative consequences.

The counsellor has already obtained a lot of information about Darren's needs deficits, and expects Darren's need to be acknowledged during his participation in the group. Based on Darren's developmental history, he may tend to become confrontational with other group members, as in fact happens:

Example: Darren

The group is attended by young men and women, aged 15-18, all of whom present with behaviours broadly similar to those displayed by Darren. While some of the young people are initially reluctant to engage with the group, and with the therapist, because they are still struggling with how to examine their transgressions without 'giving in,' Darren seems to be reluctant to participate for fear of 'sounding stupid.' Although Darren has been unhappy for a long time, he had gained some meagre satisfaction from the thought that, 'Nobody understands me; my problems are pretty special; I am different from these guys.' Darren is not always very talkative and he seems to resent how well others seem to express their own situations. In order not to feel 'left out' he responds to overt displays of emotion on the part of other group members with sarcasm. The facilitator considers that this sarcasm might represent a need to feel superior; that he knows better than they do (competency).

When Angela, a young woman who has also been 'caught' taking drugs and has quite a history of alcohol abuse talks tearfully about her need to be acknowledged by her father, who is rarely at home and has high expectations for her academic performance, Darren scoffs openly.

> *'You are just looking for attention!'* he says loudly. *'You know you are good-looking and think you can get away with anything because of it. You don't really have any problems at all!'*

Darren's comment that Angela is 'good looking' and 'thinks she can get away with anything,' actually reflects his connection to Angela's concern in that he often feels incompetent and, as a result, unacknowledged by others. But, as with his other inappropriate needs-getting behaviours, he diverts the group's attention from Angela's narrative to himself. In response, Angela turns on Darren, saying that the way she looks has 'nothing to do with it' and that Darren 'doesn't know what he is talking about' in defence of her own competency and the attention that Darren has wrested away from her and her narrative. This outcome only reinforces Darren's feelings of inadequacy in social situation and re-enforces his oppositional stance.

Although it may not have emerged in the most productive of ways, Darren's need to be acknowledged for his competency has certainly surfaced in the context of his participation in the group! Based on his developmental history, the therapist knows that Darren has the tendency to become confrontational with other group members if this need is not supported. Understanding this client's needs will benefit his treatment in at least two ways. Firstly, by highlighting this need for the client in the screening interview, both he and the counsellor will be able to anticipate the way he might react if he seems to be denied this relational requirement so that it does not become a barrier between him, the other group members and his treatment. Secondly, if he is able to discuss this within the group, the client can both practice some restraint from over-reacting to his feelings of fear or sadness at being marginalised or excluded, and can engage the group in some collaborative problem-solving around what else he can do when this situation come up for him – whether inside or outside of the group milieu. In this case, the therapist intercedes by gently saying:

> 'It seems that Darren is having difficulty in the group in the same way as Angela is at home. I am sure that many of you have felt you couldn't get it right no matter how hard you tried in certain situations.'

The creation of a good environment between group members is especially important in group work and the very process of doing so can allow the therapist and the group members to identify and explore the various universal themes that are at the root of client behaviour within the group and in the wider world.

Creating a safe group work environment in which barriers can be breached

The primary safety component in group work is respect. Regardless of the problem or problems that have brought the various group members to therapy, they must all be listened to with respect. If people sense that a group facilitator is disrespectful or that she allows group members to be disrespectful, defensive responses will arise, and these may be very damaging to the removal of barriers between the client and the ground and therapist and, indeed, any prospect for improvement. Maintaining respect for all members, and fostering respect between members, requires the group leader to acquire a high degree of objectivity towards the various people in the group.

A group maintains a safe environment by the inclusion of factors that increase safety and by the avoidance of factors that detract from safety. In feeling a sense of safety, clients can risk facing their reality as well as risking new approaches to solving their problems. But what are the factors that enhance feelings of safety? While some are related to the way the facilitator and the group members behave towards one another, others are simple and pragmatic:

Structure

Structure provides safe parameters for group work; that is, there are no surprises. Each group meeting begins with a 'sign-in,' which eases clients into group participation and ensures that each client will have his moment to be heard. During sign-in, each client is invited to provide a summary of their recent experience with the issues addressed in therapy. Providing a degree of structure, especially at the beginning of a meeting when clients are making a psychological transition from the 'real world' to the group, means that nobody has to come into the room and wonder what they should do first, and can minimise the risk of feelings of being overwhelmed or nervous from taking over. 'Signing in' gives new members an opportunity to introduce themselves and provides each member of the group the opportunity to discuss how far they have come in the course of the previous week in implementing in their daily lives the strategies that they have been discussing in therapy. The sign-in also allows treatment goal themes to emerge from the participants' sharing; this procedure also offers clients a sense of ownership in the treatment while minimising the sense of authority and direction by the therapist. In a functioning group, the sign-in evolves into an open discussion which involves members in various stages of treatment exploring the session's themes. For example, if, during the sign-in, several members express the theme of 'abandonment' and/or 'competency,' the group facilitator can 'seed' the group discussion to follow with the following emotions-focused, theme-based, statement:

> 'It seems that a number of you may be afraid that if you don't live up to other's expectations you will be left all alone.'

During the sign-in, the facilitator can respectfully intervene once a client's point has been made to prevent the client from going on too long:

Example: Sal

Sal, who has discussed his concern that others 'don't care' about his problems and that he is just a 'cog in the wheel of life' begins a litany of situations that describe his plight. Before Sal ends up dominating the entire proceedings, the therapist interjects by saying:

> 'Sal, I am sure we are relating to the sadness you must be feeling about feeling invisible in the world. Perhaps you could continue once everyone gets a chance to speak?'

In this way Sal is validated for his remarks while having an appropriate limit set by the therapist.

After the sign-in, the therapist facilitating the group assumes a low profile during the open discussion, intervening strategically and economically so as to allow the clients to 'do the work,' and closes the group by briefly summarising the session's theme. While the theme changes with each session, the format remains consistent and reliable.

Facilitation

A Needs ABC trained facilitator will sustain emotional and relational safety for group members by demonstrating high positive regard, optimism, appropriate humour, and empathy. The facilitator can intervene to help a client 'save face' if that client is struggling with feelings of embarrassment or humiliation about expressing his feelings. Certainly, a facilitator will intervene if a client is being attacked or diminished by others. A group leader models tolerance for others, as well as other appropriate relational behaviours such as communication, limit setting, negotiation, intimacy, acceptance, and flexibility.

Example: Franco

Franco, who is thirty-six, has come to group therapy because he feels that he has difficulty maintaining personal relationships. More specifically, he is lonely and feels that if he could enhance his social skills, he would be more likely to meet the life partner he so longs for. He is afraid that he is too 'set in his ways' to settle down with someone he loves although he desperately wants to and he is also afraid of admitting to how lonely he feels in case this makes him appear weak and less attractive, and in case vocalising the thought makes it 'more real.' Over the course of the first few weeks of the group, Franco reveals that he lives with his elderly mother, who still takes care of many of his needs by cooking, cleaning and ironing for him. During one group session he also fails to endear himself to female members of the group when, during an unprecedented outburst, he surprises everybody by referring to women as 'bitches,' 'crumpet,' and 'bits of fluff,' and by joking about pornography and wondering aloud how many of the other men in the group like to visit lap-dancing clubs.

For a while the group tolerates Franco, but his unacceptable behaviour continues. Just when the facilitator is about to intervene, one group member, Louise, turns to Franco with her face contorted with rage: *'Do you really think you'll ever find anyone to go out with you while you behave like that? And you must be even more stupid than I think you are if you imagine that you can talk about women that way and still find a girlfriend. You are pathetic!'*

'Yes,' adds Amanda. *'We've talked about you after meetings. We didn't really trust you before, but now I think I can speak for us all when I say that we think you should leave! You are really just a waste of space and the rest of us are here to focus on our problems.'*

At this point the group facilitator steps in: *'Come on, everybody! Franco has come to therapy, just like everybody else, because he knows he needs help. Clearly, he's stepped out of line, but I would like to remind everyone that we're here to help each other. I think Franco is struggling with the same reality that we all are: how to feel respected in relationships by being more independent and setting appropriate limits.'*

Here the facilitator acknowledges that 'competency' is an important relational need for everyone; the women in the group are feeling disrespected and are struggling with appropriate limit-setting strategies, while not considering that Franco's seemingly disrespectful attitude towards women might be because he in fact feels disrespected by them because of his apparent lack of autonomy. Franco has assessed, quite accurately, that the women think less of him because he still lives with his mother. He is sure that they do not see him as a strong, independent adult – the sort of man that a woman might like to settle down with – and attempts to field off the critical views he is sure they have by stepping in with remarks that he knows will divert them from the topic at hand.

Focus

By maintaining focus on the underlying need that has to be met, and not on the client's choice of problem-solving behaviours, clients can be encouraged to examine new, more appropriate strategies, rather than perpetrating the shame often experienced in having to come for help. In other words, even if the client has behaved reprehensibly, the role of the therapist is not to embarrass or punish them – there will be plenty of people in their everyday lives who will do that, after all – but to help them find the tools they need not to engage in the destructive behaviour again.

Each client needs to understand that, no matter what kind of perspective she feels she must maintain, it is her responsibility to eliminate the dysfunctional behaviours that have brought her to therapy, while developing new skills in order to express and deal with her feelings in more useful ways. There is also a focus on process theme; working towards identifying universal themes that describe client needs and feelings that all group members can relate to.

Focusing on feelings is often perceived by clients as validating and supportive, as we can see in the example below

Example: Gloria and Jerome

Gloria and Jerome have been married for twenty years. She had her second child about ten years ago and he claims that they have barely had sex ever since: 'Once every two or three months, if I'm lucky.' Jerome came from 'an abusive and controlling family' which he left at sixteen to get away from his mother's 'torture' ('The only time I ever saw her smile was when she had sent me to my room yet again.')

'Everything always had to be on her terms,' he said during his screening interview. *'She was only ever happy when everyone was doing what she said they had to do, no matter how miserable that made them. And now my wife is doing the same thing!'* According to Jerome, ever since their daughter was born Gloria was 'at him' to change her diapers, and even when he complied he did something wrong. Finally, after a long, drawn-out shouting match, he pushed her away. That was the point at which she called the police.

Jerome was mandated to domestic violence treatment, despite the fact he stated he had never done anything like this before. He was encouraged to examine his issues of competency and feeling of powerlessness in the group.

In his first group session, Jerome explained his situation and claimed that, even though he acknowledged that pushing Gloria was no way to solve a problem, she was 'always in his face' and 'it seemed that nothing he did was O.K.. with her.' He added: *'When I met her she was nothing like my mother. She said I was incredible, the best relationship she ever had.'* He stated that Gloria had seemed to look up to him and that she always asked his advice. Now, it seemed, she was beginning to sound like his parents–especially his father–insofar as she kept complaining that 'nothing was any good.'

At this point, the group facilitator said: *'I am sure many of us can relate to how sad it feels to be inadequate at problem-solving, especially in our important relationships'.*

Nodding, Carmine added, 'My father never thought I could do anything right, either'. Jerome continued: *'Then my wife started to say things like "Your dad was right, you mess up everything"'*.

Sylvain then piped in, saying, *'Yeah, I know just how you feel, I have been really trying to get my wife to trust me since I started coming here, but she just doesn't like anything I do for her. Even if I make her a cup of coffee, she just says it's too cold or too hot, or that I didn't put in enough sugar. I'm like, "Is she actually trying to make me mad here?"'*

Addressing the group, the group leader suggested that, *'It is a bit scary to think that you might never be trusted or appreciated again. I guess it will take a great deal of dedication to continue to prove your worth in your relationship.'*

'Boy have you got that right!' Simon immediately jumped in. 'I love my wife and my children and will never give up. It makes me very scared to think this might be a long haul but I am not a quitter.'

'You've really got my number,' interjects Lonny, who normally has to be 'pulled' into the conversation. 'I always feel that I am going to screw things up. My girlfriend keeps reminding me, too!'

In this snapshot of group process, many members were able to identify with feelings of inadequacy and fear that they will never measure up in their relationship despite the fact that their individual life situations are all different. At this point, the group facilitator suggested that the group consider possibilities for describing their feelings to their partners. They also explore potential ways in which the clients can demonstrate to themselves and their partners that they are adequate to the task ahead. Although they must take responsibility for their own behaviour, they need to learn how to express their need for trust and empowerment.

Following this suggestion, the group took part in a number of role-plays. Members took various parts, including the role of each partner, to model possibilities and strategies to help regain trust and esteem in their relationships.

Importance of emotional safety

While therapy will inevitably involve, at times, the discussion of themes and topics that make the group members feel unhappy, uncomfortable or angry, it is crucial that the group itself is experienced as a 'safe' zone. To ensure that the group remains emotionally safe for all its members, it is essential to prevent the emergence of factors that hinder effective group work. These can include the use of sarcasm that belittles a group member who is trying to open up, a focus on the specific content of a client's narrative rather than on the universal themes embedded in the narrative, confrontation and scapegoating. Let's explore an example:

Example: Angie (1)

Angie is a twenty-four year old hair stylist who is attending group therapy for an eating disorder. She reports to the group that, the previous evening, she indulged in eating two large tubs of chocolate ice cream and then felt so bad about herself that she made herself vomit.

At this point, Matt butts in: *'Yeah, my heart really bleeds for you, Angie. You are your own worst enemy. Why can't you see how stupid you are being?'*

The group falls silent, his remarks go unchecked and Angie blushes and stops talking. She stares down at her feet and twists her hands together in her lap.

Then, angrily, another group member, an older woman called Hermione adds: *'I think everyone here is making a really big effort to come to terms with their problems except Angie! She comes in every week and tells us the same old story every single time! Are we supposed to feel sorry for her? I mean, if she doesn't even try, she's just wasting everybody's time.'*

At this point, Angie bursts into tears and leaves the room, as the group breaks down into two squabbling factions; those who feel guilty about the way Angie has been treated and those who say that she has 'got what she deserved.'

Now, the role of the group facilitator is, of course, to stop such scenarios from breaking out. Angie has not been served well in the situation above and nor have any of the other members of the group. Angie is likely never to return to group therapy, and an unhealthy dynamic has been allowed to form, which may well continue for the duration of the group. While, clearly, exploring the reasons behind her behaviour is not likely to be easy for Angie or indeed for anybody else, group members need to know that the group is a safe place where they can unload their feelings and identify and discuss the reasons for them.

Maintaining reasonable levels of safety and comfort within the group will call on occasion for careful intervention and leadership from the group facilitator. Let's revisit the scene above and explore how safety could have been maintained throughout with just a little careful intervention:

Example: Angie (2)

Angie is a twenty-four year old hair stylist who is attending group therapy for an eating disorder. She reports to the group that, the previous evening, she indulged in eating two large tubs of chocolate ice cream and then felt so bad about herself that she made herself vomit.

At this point, Matt butts in: *'Yeah, my heart really bleeds for you, Angie. You are your own worst enemy. Why can't you see how stupid you are being?'*

Angie blushes and starts to get tearful. As silence falls over the group, the group worker interjects: *'I think we need to respect that, while she is not happy about what she is doing to herself, Angie trusts us enough to share her feelings and experiences with us. I think we all know how frustrating it can be to try really hard and feel that we are not getting anywhere. Perhaps some other members of the group could relate to how Angie feels and how difficult it is at times to consider other options for soothing their wounds.'*

At this point another group member, an older woman called Hermione, adds: *'It really upsets me to have to hear Angie telling us the same thing every week. It makes me feel scared because I start thinking that the challenge I'm facing is too big for me, as well.'*

A difficult moment has passed, a challenge to feelings of safety within the group has been deflected, and the theme of competency embedded in the specific content of Angie's narrative has been generalised to the group, leaving open the possibility of discussion of other member's experiences and the ability to risk self-disclosure. Now group members can relate to how difficult it is, in fact, for a 'quick fix' to happen and to Angie's reality that putting into practice what they have learned is difficult under the best of circumstances. As well, they can address the importance of feeling safe enough to disclose even if they have 'fallen off the wagon' and understand the importance of working together to find 'new and improved' problem-solving strategies.

Challenges to emotional group safety

Generally, the following can be categorised as situations that can compromise the emotional safety of a group, and that should be avoided:

- *One-on-one case work:* One way a group can easily become bogged down is for the facilitator to engage in extended one-on-one conversations with a client during a group session;

- *Sarcasm*: While there is a great need for humour and lightness at times in all groups, there is absolutely no room for sarcasm. Sarcasm reflects judgmental attitudes and is invariably perceived as a threatening and demeaning;

- *Excessive focus on content*: Focusing on the mere content of client's narratives, or justification of rightness or fault, can be perceived as judgmental and/or punitive, and counter-indicate the development of a trusting relationship between client and therapist. Instead, a focus on the feelings that are implied in the content of the client's narrative, and the process theme embedded therein, will encourage the client by validating what their struggle is really about.

- *Confronting versus challenging the client*: It is important that clients do not perceive themselves as being singled out by the facilitator. Supportively challenging, through constructive feedback, the behavioural problems and not confronting the person's attitude or personality, minimises the threat of derision and stigmatisation;

- *Scapegoating*: One way that group members can acquire a false sense of safety is to scapegoat another member. When clients take a holiday from working on their own issues by singling out a group member to 'work on,' they avoid the important aspects of the treatment process: self-evaluation, personal responsibility and development of empathy.

Challenges to emotional client safety

Fear of change is a feeling that is frequently expressed by people attending group therapy, even though they have come to therapy in an attempt to change behavioural patterns that may well have been making them very unhappy for a long time. Often, dysfunctional behaviours are so much a part of the identity of the person who is displaying them that there is a very real fear that they will not be the 'the same person' if these behaviours are eliminated. The facilitator needs to reassure group members that they can and will be the same people even when they have learned how to deal with their problems differently. Let's look at an example:

Example: Natasha

Natasha is an attractive woman in her thirties who married at just twenty to a significantly older man who supported her and their three children financially and in every other way, including paying for a series of nannies to take care of the little ones, leaving Natasha free to do whatever she wanted. When she was widowed, Natasha found herself having to fill a strong role in her family, especially as her husband died in strained financial circumstances, and Natasha no longer has as much money as she used to.

Natasha is finding widowhood very difficult, as she was used to being the 'pretty, dependent, fluffy-headed' one, who was able to relax in the knowledge that she would always be taken care of, just as she was always taken care of by her doting parents, who were fond of saying, *'Natasha is just so pretty, everyone is always going to want to take care of her!'* Because she felt herself to be 'the always cared for person,' and was always under the assumption that people would inevitably come to her assistance and 'do for her,' Natasha has never had to carry out tasks like balancing a cheque-book and is not sure that she knows how. Also, Natasha has long enjoyed a 'party lifestyle' and has developed a serious cocaine habit. If she is to deal with her substance abuse, she will have to accept that she is an adult person and that it is no longer appropriate for her to assume that there will always be someone there to pick up the tab, psychologically as well as financially.

From Natasha's participation in the group process the facilitator considers that since her need for reliability was met in childhood and adolescence by being cared for by her parents in her earlier development, and that doing things for herself had not been a consideration until now, Natasha's lack of felt 'competency' is an important treatment issue for her. Thus, the facilitator can link her to other members of the group who seem to have similar concerns with a statement like: *'I guess there are many of you who doubt their abilities to problem-solve without someone's help.'* Or: *'I am sure many of you can relate to Natasha with regard to "going it alone"'*.

The group leader can also intervene around the reality that you can not use cocaine and still have fun: *'I wonder whether anyone can relate to the frustration that with the substance abuse problems you have you might not be able to enjoy any more good times?'* In this way, the facilitator encourages members to share similar concerns or the reality that 'good times' do not necessarily have to involve drugs; that effective problem-solving is better done with a 'clear head' and that not using under duress is a sign of competency in and of itself.

Supportive challenges

When group members relate in an empathic rather than a critical way to what is being expressed by one of them, a sense of safety and connection develops. Often, in empathising with other clients in the group, members are, in effect, projecting some of their own anxieties and emotions. Let's look at an example:

Example: Fred

Fred has been mandated to group therapy because he has difficulty in controlling his tendency towards violence, which he has often used against his wife Anja. He tends to try to justify his violent episodes by highlighting things that annoy him about his Anja's behaviour.

'What really got me going this week,' Fred says, *'was when Anja went swanning off to the hairdresser to get her hair done – with my money – and came back three hours later. I mean, how long does it take to get your hair done? For all I know, she got her hair done first and then went to see the*

Chippendales with her stupid friends. She's always going out and doing things and never comes back when she says she will! It doesn't matter if I've arranged for babysitters so we can go out or if I have cooked supper. She doesn't care if she screws it up! It's as if she is actually trying to make me as angry as she can.'

John, another member of the group, leans forward in his chair. *'You know, my wife does the exactly same sort of thing,'* he interjects. *'This weekend she told me she would spend the day with me; we were going to go and choose new curtains for the den. She'd been nagging me for ages to come up with the money for them and I had finally given in. I was about to get ready to leave and she told me she had to go to her manicurist. Her manicurist! She had made the appointment long ago and forgotten to tell me. Or so she said. I mean, how important can her nails be, for God's sake?'*

Both men shake their heads in mock resignation as the therapist asks: *'I wonder if any of you can connect to what John and Fred are saying?'*

After a moment's thought, Ahmed, another member of the group, says: *'Yeah, my wife's card games with the girls are more important than being with me! She's always getting out of things by saying: "Oh, I forgot to tell you, I'm going over to Clara's to play cards so I can't go with you"'.*

There is a long silence and then John begins to describe that he often feels unimportant in his relationship, and asks Fred if he agrees.

'Yeah,' agrees Fred. *'But that's not all. There's more to it than that. I mean, a hairdresser is just someone you pay for a service. If I've planned a nice evening together, surely that should matter more?'*

'You guys sound really jealous!' Steve, who has been silent until now, blurts out. *'I think you are jealous because you feel as though your wives want to spend more time with other people than with you, even people they don't really know. Why can't you just tell them how you feel – that you wonder why the others are so important – without getting mad? Maybe they'll even like it.'*

Fred and John agree that they could try this.

'Women like to feel that they are valued,' John adds thoughtfully.

'I suppose everyone does,' Fred agrees. There is some laughter in the group in recognition that an important understanding has been stated.

A model for group work and other psychotherapies

This technique of helping clients to focus on relational needs makes it easier for additional clients to 'join in' promoting group interaction and generally mitigating the potential for clients to feel that they cannot relate to others in the group, as well as any potential power differential, both among group members and between the group and the facilitator, by avoiding inappropriate challenges to client behaviour. It also has the potential to enlist each member as a 'co-therapist' in advocating better strategies than the dysfunctional behaviours that they have been displaying in real life; it promotes each member's own use of empathy and insight to think self-critically in interacting with other group members. This form of supportive challenging and self-evaluation, in turn, can be transferred into situations outside of the group. Finally, being 'in the driver's seat' is an effective way to encourage the assimilation of appropriate problem-solving strategies.

Humour, particularly self-directed humour on the part of the group leader, can be a valuable tool in doing group work. For example, in a group where the topic of discussion is fear of making a mistake in attempting to accomplish a goal, for the facilitator to say, 'I was wrong once. It was in 1976...I think it was a Thursday,' does much to reduce feelings of vulnerability and inadequacy among group members. Humour is a constructive way to break the tension after an emotionally rife interchange; humour helps a client to 'lighten up' which, in turn, encourages a client to open up. Humour has a quality that can draw out reluctant clients and supportively challenge defended clients without being threatening. Humorous interventions[39] are often effective in bringing underlying emotional themes to the surface. For example, if clients in a group session continue to discuss their anxiety at being abandoned or rejected, a facilitator, who has remained quiet for some time, could say: 'I wonder if you would mind my saying something at this point because *I'm* beginning to feel a little rejected.' The resulting laughter could indicate that the underlying emotion has been illuminated to the group in a gentler, less obvious, way. The facilitator could then add: 'It sounds to me like everyone here feels rejected.'

While bonding among group members is important, bonding around constructive themes is clearly to be advised, rather than around the problems that have brought them into therapy in the first place. As one of the axioms of the Needs ABC is that the focus remain on the therapeutic unit (in this case the group), and the individual clients who comprise it, knowing when or how to intervene, and when more active versus more passive intervention is appropriate, is a delicate task. We shall now turn our attention to this important point.

8
How and when to intervene

FOR A POSITIVE THERAPEUTIC outcome, it is important that the facilitator is viewed positively by her clients. This in turn depends to a large extent on whether or not she has successfully intervened in assisting her clients to explore the issues at the core of their problematic behaviours. But, at the same time, knowing when to withdraw from a group's interaction is just as important as knowing when to interject. Intervention is not always good.

Key to an affective application of the Needs ABC model is that clients must come to understand when and how they themselves must take responsibility for their own feelings, by interacting productively with the other members of the group, with their family members or spouse or, in the case of individual therapy, with the therapist herself.

Although it is essential that clients use therapy to acquire the tools they need to explore their own emotions, during therapy the facilitator should always have her hand on the rudder, even if the pressure she applies in 'steering' the group is subtle and beneath the water.

The power of the therapist

It is important for a therapist to maintain safety and control while also retaining the ability to 'fade into the background' when it is apparent that the group has developed a momentum of its own, and is using this momentum to explore productive avenues. The therapist is, of course, in a position of authority. It can be tempting for him to allow himself to become a little intoxicated by his situation and, however subtly, to allow the group to begin to focus on him. However, because of the strong position that a facilitator inherits by virtue of her function, it is important that this authority remain functional and positive in maintaining her clients' focus on survival and healing rather than on indulging in feelings of victimisation or distraction from their goals. In achieving this end, it is helpful to remember that interventions do not have to occur immediately as issues evolve.

Tracking each member of a therapeutic unit, and storing the information for future reference, can result in timely interventions that impact in an economical and positive way for everybody concerned. Let's look at a case study illustrating this:

Example: George

During the 'sign-in' of in a substance abuse treatment group, George, a group member, stated that his friends were extremely important to him though when he did spend time with them he would find himself 'forced' into having 'just one drink' which would lead inevitably to an 'all-nighter' and the hang-over, guilt and recrimination that inexorably followed. At this point, other group members seemed to use their sign-in to place the blame of their substance use on others, as George had done. By tracking individual member process, the facilitator realised that a fear of being marginalised or discounted by others (a theme that had come up in the past) was embedded in these group members' statements.

When the sign-in was completed the facilitator said: 'Many of you seem to be describing how scary it is to feel 'left out' when you are with your friends or loved ones. Do any of you have any thoughts as to how you could feel more included with those you care about without using?'

By vocalising his observations about group members' reactions without directing his comments at any one person in particular, the facilitator has redirected the group members to take responsibility for their behaviours while helping them to understand some of the emotional possibilities inherent in their statements.

Initially, the facilitator must help the client to connect to the setting and to the group process, experiencing a sense of safety that can lead to greater participation and self-disclosure. Once a sense of security has been developed, the next goal is for the client to take responsibility for his problem and collaborate with the leader and other participants in the development of appropriate strategies. The facilitator must also assess a client's emotional states during the group work process and help them to understand what their emotions represent and how they arose in the course of their emotional development.

Helping the group member to join

Engaging all participants in the group process to some extent is extremely important; if some members of the group remain peripheral to the discussion of issues and problem-solving strategies, while others are too active and take up too much space, the dynamic of the whole group can be negatively affected. Those who are quiet may leave the group with reinforced negative feelings about their own ability to interact with others. ('If I can't even cope with a therapy session set up for people like me, how am I supposed to cope in the real world?') Those who are overly active might end up learning nothing about appropriate limits or how to collaborate with others ('As long as I do what I need to for myself things will work out for me, so who cares about the others?') That said, a careful approach is essential.

The facilitator must be aware of individual limitations in order to avoid what the participant might perceive as coercive, potentially silencing him. A 'quiet' or inactive member may be one who is new to the group, who may lack the confidence of others in the group or who could be described as 'oppositional,' 'defensive' or 'dug-in.' The facilitator must use supportive and encouraging strategies to help engage this individual. Briefly, a client's beliefs and behaviours cannot be challenged before he has gained some confidence in the group. Linking this person to other group members, or helping him to feel included in the group itself is key. Let's take a look at an example:

Aside from seeming to struggle with her first group sign-in in a substance abuse treatment facility, Jane has been silent throughout most of the group. Linda (another group member) has just discussed her anger at Youth Protection Services, which forced her to place her children with her sister until she is better able to care for them. Linda is bitter, angry, and embarrassed about her situation. The group leader recalls that Jane has also been placed under similar conditions and (turning to Jane) says: 'Jane, you have been pretty quiet until now and I was wondering if you can connect in some way to what Linda was saying?'

Needs ABC: Acquisition and Behaviour Change

Here, the group leader has placed control of the process entirely with Jane, giving her an opportunity to comment on any part of Linda's statement, or even to refute the leader's intervention. The way in which Jane responds to this intervention will not only help her to vocalise her views and discuss her problems, but will also provide clues as to the universal themes underlying her own behaviours. For example, suppose that Jane says:

> 'I don't think it's the same at all. It sounds as though Linda just wasn't coping with her kids' demands. But I'm not having any difficulties – not serious ones, anyway. I can keep the two areas of my life separate! I have never let my kids see me when I am using. So far as they are concerned, I'm just your average soccer mom.'

On the face of it, Jane seems to be very resistant to change and even to the idea that there is anything about her behaviour that warrants change at all. But the narrative above reveals a fear of powerlessness insofar as Jane appears to 'protest too much' when, in fact, she clearly is struggling with her personal life, as well as a need for respect as a mother and as a human being – a fear of being regarded as incompetent. Notwithstanding Jane's apparent resistance to accepting her own dilemmas vis a vis parenting and substance abuse, she has provided enough information about herself to give the facilitator and the other group members an 'in' to request more information about her. Here the group worker could say, for example: 'I'm sure many of you can understand how Jane feels. It must be frustrating only to have your faults pointed out and not your successes.'

The group worker must be able to understand member behaviour and interpret process theme. For example, a group member who initially presents with a highly intellectualised position, focusing on what others have done to him is, at first glance, playing the role of 'victim.' This role can be frustrating for a group facilitator and can lead to futile efforts at helping to move the group member out of this position. A group member in substance abuse treatment, for example, who states during her sign-in that she had relapsed because she stopped attending AA meetings and that 'otherwise everything else seemed to be going O.K.' can also be saying that she has a fear of being betrayed by the group, difficulty trusting in others, a concern that she will be ridiculed or be too problematic to be helped and a need for a formula to support her attempts to change because of her own frustration with a lack of understanding about why she continues to be unable to fend off relapse. If the facilitator recalls that, during the assessment interview, the client mentioned that she had been verbally and physically assaulted and demeaned by her parents, the group leader could empathically say: 'I am sure the group understands how difficult it has been for you to trust anyone by asking for their help.' This statement also tacitly invites the client to consider reaching out for help and sharing details about her background.

Process theme versus content

It is invariably more helpful to focus on process theme (group and individual) rather than content in order to promote objectivity on the part of the therapist. Labelling a client who presents as 'oppositional' or challenging a 'troublemaker' can prevent empathic interventions as the selection of such a term, even if it is never articulated by the therapist, has created an obstacle to real change. Conversely, a compassionate statement can help to maintain client safety and helps with self-disclosure as well as modelling similar responses from the group. Crucially, one maintains focus on the reasons behind problematic behaviours and statements, and not the behaviours and statements themselves.

But therapists are human beings too, and if they fall prey to feeling injured or challenged they must be careful that they are able to identify, isolate, and maintain control of their emotions. For example, a client who challenges the group facilitator by saying: 'I really don't like the way you are running this group,' may elicit thoughts such as: 'Maybe he's right and I'm not doing good work,' or 'What a pompous jerk!' On the other hand, by examining the theme behind what appeared to be a rather scathing, personal comment, the following interpretations can be made: 'Don't get too close,' 'Go easy on me,' or, 'I'm frightened.'

In this case, the following supportive interventions could be made: 'I know the group understands how difficult it has been for you to come to this treatment,' or 'Does anyone else here feel uneasy about trusting the group?' This will provide another opportunity to discover client relational needs with regard to trusting others. A secondary benefit of turning the apparently aggressive statement over to the group may be to give the facilitator a moment to 'cool down' and consider the statement in the context of the therapeutic session, rather than as an attack on her.

Timing

It is unlikely that all clients will arrive at the same level or 'phase' simultaneously. In other words, some people will be able to begin constructively exploring their own behaviours and emotions and implement new strategies in their daily relational interactions before others. This is perfectly normal and should not be a cause of concern to anybody. While this can seem challenging, it is not a problem, even in the context of a closed group with a specific time frame. In fact, those who are ready to explore their behaviours and emotions earlier can positively model a constructive engagement in therapy to group members who are more ambivalent about exposing their inner selves.

However, the fact that client movement does not occur at uniform rates means that facilitators must evaluate each participant's progress before planning their interventions. While respecting the group's momentum, the leader can be overtly involved in the group when it is active. During this period, it is important for the group leader to witness the evolution of group and individual process in order to avoid making premature statements provoked by the witnessing of inappropriate group activity such as scapegoating, defocusing, intellectualising, etc. Let's explore an example:

Example: A survivors' support group

A survivors' support group has been involved in a discussion about their anger at and fear of not being able to trust family members. Sylvie, a group member who had previously disclosed feelings of disconnection from her family has not, as yet, entered the discussion. The group leader, having noticed this, waits for an appropriate break in the discussion, turns to the group and says (with a linking intervention): 'It seems to me that Sylvie and Henry seem somewhat alike in their view of family.'

During the brief silence that follows Sylvie appears restless at first and then cautiously says: 'Yes, I suppose Henry and I come from pretty similar family backgrounds. But he seems to be able to talk more freely about how he feels when his parents doubt his ability to get on. I still get so hurt that I just can't talk and I end up getting back into my shell and staying there!'

'Believe me, I still feel that way sometimes,' Henry comments. 'But I have found a few ways that help me to speak out...'

'Well, anything you can give me here would be great,' Sylvie responds. 'Maybe it'll work and maybe it won't but I am really stuck for ideas on my own.'

Therapist self-disclosure

Appropriate self-disclosure can be used by the leader to animate the group by modelling self-disclosure, but it must be exercised with caution! Therapist self-disclosure is a powerful tool and can be a model for group members in building safety, for taking responsibility and promoting interaction, but there is the risk of moving the group focus from group interaction to the facilitator, diminishing group momentum. Although the therapist's observations from his own experience can be useful, the group is not meeting to discuss his problems.

Having said that, carefully employed therapist self-disclosure can also be used to help to create a sense of responsibility and cohesion among group members, as well as highlighting particular issues that might be overlooked by the participants. Let's look at an example:

Example: Fred

Fred (a participant in a survivors' group) describes his concern that he is constantly fearful of doing something wrong in his relationships (work, friends, and partner) – that he is invariably the one to blame when something goes wrong. There is a silence in the group and the therapist, noticing some heads nodding in agreement, enters the discussion by saying: *'I know just how you feel. One day I came home and found my partner looking very down and the first thing I thought was, 'On no! What did I do?' I often worry that the long hours I work mean that he's having to spend evenings on his own too much and that he's angry with me for not making more 'us' time. This time, however, I asked him, "What's up?," and discovered that it wasn't me at all but that his boss was giving him a hard time. I am sure we have all had similar experiences.'*

With this appropriate exposure of self, the group facilitator has normalised the experience of self-doubt as well as having demonstrated an appropriate problem-solving option. Self-disclosure does, of necessity, involve sharing such personal information. Consider the following simple piece of self-disclosure that tacitly invites clients to share information:

'Well, the holiday season is coming up. I can't speak for you guys, but for me the pressure of having to put on a good face all the time can be really stressful, and sometimes at this time of year the old frustrations I used to feel towards others seem to bubble up to the surface. I'm telling you, every time my father-in-law says the turkey is too dry it reminds me of how resistant he was to my marrying his daughter–even though we've actually had a pretty good relationship for years!'

In this case, the therapist's disclosure is received with nods of recognition on the part of the group members who chime in with observations like the following:

'I know exactly what you mean. All the things that drive me nuts about my father are even worse at Christmas because everyone's expectations of fun are so high. When he starts becoming a control freak and trying to organise the unwrapping of presents, it's the last straw!'

'Hey, don't think you Christians have a monopoly on awkward festivals. During Ramadan, my family fasts all day and has a big meal every evening–the whole family, together. It should be nice but when we're all at my house, my sister keeps reminding me that I use readymade meals, unlike her oh-so-perfect homemade stuff and the friction that there always was between us when we were growing up just comes right back.'

'Think that's bad? Because my Mom and Dad became Jehovah's Witnesses. That means we get all the tension of the holiday season, when everyone's together and off work–but we don't even get to celebrate and open presents!'

Helping group members to take responsibility

Many people who come to therapy are there at least in part because they have not learned how to be responsible for their own behaviour, and key to developing healthy ways in which to respond to the meaningful others in their lives is helping them to take responsibility for all their behaviours, negative and positive. In the context of therapy using the Needs ABC model, various strategies have been found to help members to take responsibility for their presenting problems:

Maintaining the group's focus on its mandate

Maintaining the group focus on its mandate is an important way of preventing potentially problematic behaviours such as scapegoating, 'bashing' and defocusing. Allowing the group to stray from time to time – for example, tolerating discussion of current affairs, the weather, the problems of people who are not in the group or other general issues that defocus from the topic mandate of the group – can give the facilitator some useful information on group process theme and world-view, but it can also help group members to avoid important and potentially therapeutic issues while building a 'negative momentum' that may become difficult to stop. For example:

Example: Jerry

Jerry, in a domestic violence treatment group, has described that even though he understands he should not have pushed his partner out of the way when he became angry, she has often pushed him aside physically when she becomes upset, too.

'O.K., so I pushed her. I'm not saying that that's right. But what about all the times she's shoved me out of the way? Once, she almost slammed the car door closed on my hand. On purpose, too! But now she's sitting at home watching soap operas and being self-righteous to her sister on the phone and I'm missing my weekly poker game to come here! I guess she reckons she can be as mean as she likes and that's just fine and dandy!'

Cleve, a somewhat defended group member, immediately jumps in and says: *'That's always the way it is. It's O.K. for women to hit us, but we so much as look at a chick the wrong way and we are the ones who are wrong – never them.'*

Simon pipes in: *'Yeah, what about what they do? They are the ones who need to be here.'*

Most of the men in the group start to shift in their chairs and it is obvious that they all have an axe to grind, but before anyone else gets a chance to join them, the group leader says: *'Even though we all know that two wrongs don't make a right,, I understand that it can be tough to focus on our part in a wrongdoing. Maybe some of the women in your lives would also benefit from therapy, but they're not here right now. I wonder whether any of you can suggest some strategies to Jerry that might be more helpful than what he has done.'*

Rather than lecturing to, or criticising the two speakers for women bashing, the leader has brought the group back to its behavioural mandate with a focus on member insight and without perpetuating the attempted shift in focus.

Giving group members information about their behaviour

Information-giving to promote insight and behaviour change is an important aspect of therapy, including didactic components and information-giving, as well as group member insight gained, interpretations and conclusions. For example:

Example: Sarah

Sarah, who is in an inpatient substance abuse treatment centre for the third time, told the group (with some despair in her voice) that even though she had done better this time it seemed that everyone she knew was abusing drugs of one form or another.

'I was clean almost nine months this time around, but I just can't seem to escape my friends who use. Everyone I know is on drugs – there's just nowhere for me to go. My parents are dead and my sister won't talk to me.'

At this point the group leader stated to the group: *'All of you seem to recognise periods of abstinence and we know from doing research that the percentage of people that remains clean goes up with every treatment they take. Perhaps some of you could respond to Sarah with this in mind.'*

Information-giving interventions, as in the example above, can help the clients to understand that there is a difference between what they perceive and what is factual (reality testing) while respectfully challenging their misconceptions.

A model for group work and other psychotherapies

Facilitating group discussion and dialogue

Facilitation of discussion and dialogue amongst group participants is a key element of the leader's role, and can also function as a metaphor for responsibility taking. When a client engages in rather than withdraws from a discussion, they are acquiring a skill that they can bring to the greater world; one that they will be able to use in forging more healthy ways of responding to their emotional needs. The Needs ABC approach emphasises the importance of dialogue, or 'peer counselling.' For example:

Example: Jennifer

Jennifer, a relatively new member of a single mothers' group, had been quiet during the first half of the group session and appears to be more interested in looking at the posters on the walls than in engaging with the group.

The therapist remembered from Jennifer's intake interview that she had many issues around loyalty, reliability and betrayal not only in her now defunct marriage, but also in her family of origin. Some of the other women had been lamenting about 'never seeing it coming' and 'being left high and dry' with regard to the end of their relationship with their respective husbands. At this point in time the counsellor said: 'Jennifer, I was wondering whether you can relate in any way to what these women are talking about?'

In this example, the facilitator has encouraged Jennifer to take some responsibility for herself by asking her to join in with the rest of the group. The intervention was purposefully made in a non-specific way with the hope that Jennifer might select something by herself that she gleaned from the group. Any comment Jennifer makes, no matter how trivial it might seem, would be supported and validated with regard to her participation in the group. Supportive challenging can be done gradually, as Jennifer becomes more comfortable in her ability to participate. In this case, Jennifer says:

'I think even worse than the fact that Mike left me was the fact that he had been lying to me about caring about me for ages before he left. All those times he brought home flowers or took me out to dinner…he had already decided that he was going to leave, so it was just a mockery. He was just making fun of me and I didn't even realise it. All my happiest memories from the good

years of the marriage have been poisoned. Even when I think about when our son Jamie was born – Mike was late arriving to the hospital. He didn't even make it on time to cut the umbilical cord, although the weekend before he had found time to spend a night in Las Vegas with that slut from the office. Now I think we mattered so little he just didn't care.'

Here the therapist could comment to the group: 'Jennifer brings up an excellent theme here with regard to feeling invisible in important relationships.'

This intervention not only validated Jennifer's participation but opens up a topic that others can reflect on, and that may help them to gain insight into their own personal situations.

Assessing the group member's emotional state

It is also essential to assess clients' emotional states in light of what they describe to the group, bearing in mind that the emotions expressed are frequently not the same as those felt, and are inferred 'between the lines' of the client's dialogue. Teaching the client about emotional possibilities is important and helpful, especially in the case of clients who never learned or understood what basic emotional states are because of the defences used in their survival and potential concerns about vulnerability, those who understand that they have feelings but are confused about how to label them, and those who are very concrete in their thinking, such as members with cognitive difficulties or limited educational backgrounds. It is worth noting that men frequently use terms such as 'anger' to describe fear or anxiety, while women often do the opposite (although of course it is important not to generalise unduly) Let's explore an example:

Example: Solomon

Solomon, during a substance abuse treatment clinic sign-in, described an incident between himself and his partner wherein she told him that she was not sure that she could trust him not to drink at a wedding they had been invited to.

'It really pisses me off that my wife still doesn't trust me even though I have been in treatment for over a month now,' he said. 'Eventually I persuaded her that we should go. Then I was trying to relax and have a good time at

her cousin's wedding even though I could only drink Coca-Cola, but she kept giving me a beady-eyed stare the whole time until I bet everyone in the room knew what she was thinking! It's so humiliating to be treated like a dog on a short chain.'

The facilitator replied: *'I am sure many can relate to how scary it is to think of how long it might take to earn back your wife's trust.'*

By reframing the anger ('pissed off') with fear ('scary') in a matter-of-fact and non-judgemental way, the group leader is able to show empathy and teach an emotional possibility for that incident, while also showing the client that it is normal and acceptable for him, a man, to be afraid of 'facing his demons' and embracing change.

Eliciting clients' emotionally based suggestions tends not to disrupt momentum as much as several statements aimed at individual clients. It can engage the group in a dialogue and it encourages self-discovery and peer mentoring. Here is another example:

Example: Willa

Willa, attending a domestic violence survivors' group, tearfully described how desperately hard she had tried to meet her partner's wishes: *'I don't understand it, I did everything he asked. I knew I wouldn't be able to stay much longer – but I never thought he would actually hit me after all I had done for him. He said he preferred blondes to brunettes so I even dyed my hair for him, and I was always on a diet because he thought I was too fat. I've been hungry for years. I'm still afraid of him even though now I live in a different city.'*

One of the co-facilitators turned to the group and said: *'It must be very frustrating for Willa to have stayed so long…only to find that she had no choice but to leave. Would any of you care to share with the group how you would feel in Willa's situation?'*

In this way the group is encouraged to become involved in a discussion around the emotional component of Willa's story.

In this case, Natasha chimes in: *'Yeah, you feel like you've wasted a big chunk of your life. And for what? Nothing! I gave Adrian my twenties and thirties – the best years of my life! And all I got in return was abuse. Thanks for nothing, Adrian.'*

How the facilitator might feel in a particular situation presented by the group can be suggested if there are additional possibilities for feelings that have not been mentioned in any emotionally-focussed exercise or dialogue, or if the facilitator believes that the feeling descriptions presented have been inadequate. Let's look at an example:

Example: Abstinence group

In a relatively 'young' closed gambling treatment group the members were having a discussion around the struggle that they were having with abstinence and their difficulty in regaining support and trust from friends and family. The facilitator had tried to direct the group towards a discussion of how this made them feel, but most of the members were insistent on blaming others for emotions that were contributing to their relapse. At this point, the facilitator said:

'I have two minds about how I would be feeling if I was in your situation. On the one hand I would feel extremely frustrated and sad at not getting the emotional support from others that I needed; on the other hand, I would be much more frightened – perhaps terrified – that I would never be able to beat this thing and be lonely and miserable for the rest of my life. Any thoughts about what I have said?'

This 'quasi self-disclosure' helps to bring some emotional options to the floor that may be difficult for the group to examine. It is a way of challenging the group member's world-view while normalising it as an acceptable emotional experience, and providing a vocabulary that can be used in discussion.

Structured group exercises

Structured group exercises can be a useful tool when the group appears to be becoming chaotic, interrupting inappropriate group member interactions or dialogue and modelling a 'time-out' or limit-setting skill used to gain perspective on a difficult situation:

Example: Domestic violence group

In a domestic violence treatment group, a male and a female co-therapy team encountered a sense that the group was gradually becoming less and less in control. George, one of the group members, had suggested that his partner was making it impossible for him to feel successful even though she knew how hard it was for him to go for help: *'I am doing what I am supposed to do, but she still gets angry with me.'*

With this, Ted jumped in saying: *'Yeah, all women can do is criticise. When we begin to do well, they find some other way of putting us down.'* The group seemed to be dividing itself into two camps, one in support of the partner's position and one in support of Ted's perspective.

At this point, one of the group leaders said: *'O.K., guys. Grab your feeling charts. Now, we are going to go around the room and I would like each one of you, by selecting from the feelings on the chart, to tell us how and what you would be feeling, and why, if you were George.'*

This 'reaching for feelings' intervention is a way of reapplying group norms and values by redirecting the interaction and thereby 'gently' interrupting the potential for defocusing from the therapeutic goals or scapegoating the victims of the violence or the group members themselves.

Of course, each facilitator will find their own way of expressing their style of leadership and personality within the context of the Needs ABC approach, and there is considerable scope for flexibility within the Needs ABC guidelines, provided that one remembers to share all issues with the group rather than making interventions to an individual, that group leader interventions can lead to a decrease in group momentum and should be used sparingly and wisely, and that the leader should attempt to intervene only after the group has developed sufficient interpersonal dialogue between group members so that they will have the impetus to continue following the facilitator's comments.

Helping the involuntary client

Many people are sent to therapy for one reason or another, including perpetrators of domestic or sexual abuse and alcohol and other substance abusers, with 'sent' being the operative word. Typical examples would include the man who has been told that he must address his problems with domestic violence before he is allowed access to his children, or the drug addict who has been sent to group therapy following apprehension for theft. Sometimes, men and women already serving prison sentences are also 'sentenced' to group therapy on a 'plea bargain' to shorten their jail time. This can put the therapist in the rather awkward situation of being viewed as being in the same camp as prison guards, judges and other figures of authority, a view that will have to be overcome if the client is to truly benefit from therapy.

Many, if not most, therapy participants are already profoundly ambivalent about attending therapy in the first place. This is even truer of those who are mandated to therapy. The lack of volition on their part can add to their reluctance to trust or participate in their treatment, especially if they see it as part of their punishment. They may think, 'It was bad enough when my wife got the restraining order, but now I am going to have to give up my spare time to go and talk about feelings and other 'mumbo jumbo',' or worry, 'Is this a trick to get me to say something that will get me into even more trouble? How do I know that this guy is not going to go and talk to the lawyers or prison warden about me when the session is over? What if I say that I get mad sometimes and they use that as an excuse not to consider me for parole when the time comes?'

Helping such involuntary clients to make the most of therapy poses particular challenges. However, a careful touch can turn negatives into positives, by using these very feelings of being punished to explore deeper reasons behind the client's presence in the group.

Let's look at the case of a man who has been sent to group therapy because of his repeatedly abusive, violent behaviour towards his wife:

Example: Scully

Scully, a white-collar worker, is currently in the throes of divorce. He and his wife, Linda, have two children. Linda is seeking sole custody of the children on the grounds that Scully is an unsuitable role model and is violent towards her. If Scully is to have any sustained contact with his children at all, he will have to attend therapy and demonstrate that he has really changed the way he behaves. Although Scully's love of his children is certainly real, he makes no secret of the fact that he believes that therapy is 'a load of voodoo bullshit' and that he believes himself to be the real victim in this scenario, although he admits that he has hit Linda on numerous occasions, even causing her substantial injury more than once, 'When she provoked it...she knew what she was doing!.'

'I'm here because of my kids,' Scully says defensively during the first group session. *'I really love them and if they say I have to come here once a week for however long, I suppose I'll just have to do it. The whole legal system is on the side of women, anyway. You're damned if you do, and damned if you don't. The 'feminazis' have a stranglehold in this country.'*

Scully's body language is defensive, with arms crossed and a rather belligerent expression on his face. It is not easy for the therapist to feel any immediate sense of sympathy for this wife-beater. However, even the few words that Scully has uttered provide some insight into the unmet needs that lie behind his deeply unpleasant maladaptive behaviour.

In stating that he feels that one is 'damned if you do, and damned if you don't,' Scully is revealing a fear of change, as well as the fear that he may be unable to create the change in himself that is necessary for him to be allowed to see his children. It is clear that Scully is grappling with issues related to feelings of powerlessness and doubts about his competency. But a chink of optimism is also present when he says that he will 'do it if he has to.' Scully is inviting the therapist and the group to help him, even as he expresses his fear of change and reluctance to investigate his own motivations and behaviour. An empathic group intervention could be the way to go when Scully describes his scepticism at being in the group; such as: 'I am sure we all can relate to worrying about if we will be able do what others ask from us, especially after completing treatment.'

The situation facing the therapist who is dealing with Hortensia, a woman who has been sent to therapy even as she serves a prison sentence seems even more difficult:

Example: Hortensia

Hortensia is serving a sentence for negligent homicide after failing to seek medical attention for her child, who was clearly ill and who died following a ruptured appendix. Hortensia was high on drugs at the time of the child's illness and failed to react appropriately to the situation. Currently, her other children have been placed in care, and Hortensia's attorneys are appealing her case. Hortensia has come off drugs, and has been advised by her attorneys that her case has a much greater chance of success if she is seen to be taking proactive steps towards getting better. Wracked with grief and feelings of guilt, Hortensia feels that she has already been 'punished enough by God' and is attending therapy only under duress.

'Nothing I can do will bring Harley back to life,' she says in an early session. *'But it's not my fault he's gone. Maybe I could have done more, but ultimately it was fate, and fate is cruel. The authorities have made a terrible situation even worse by taking me away from my other four kids. I can't bear to think of them in foster homes and I know that they are very unhappy without their mom. Why did they take them away? You can't make a right with two wrongs!'*

Again, while Hortensia states her opposition to attending therapy, her narrative provides the facilitator with an 'in.' By stating that 'maybe' she could have done more, she is indicating her willingness to accept responsibility for her drug abuse, and by stressing her love for her surviving children, she shows that she is determined to improve her situation. The group facilitator could suggest the following to the group in this case: *'Wow, I am sure we all understand how much courage it takes to admit your wrongs and to show others that you are committed to meeting your responsibilities.'*

In approaching therapy from the perspective of the Needs ABC model, it is always important to help the client realise that, once she recognises the unmet emotional needs that lie behind her maladaptive behaviour, she already has the power to change. It is especially important to make this message clear to involuntary clients who are serving time in a penal institution, who may associate their therapist with the authorities who have put them 'behind bars.' In these circumstances, it is not unusual for clients to resist self-disclosure and candour in order to feel some power in the light of the loss of power and control they are currently experiencing. This stance effectively prevents them from getting better and it is crucial to find a way to circumvent it.

While key to helping involuntary clients is the therapist's ability to help them to identify their own unmet emotional needs – probably for the first time – and figure out a better way to meet them, some practical issues can help to foster a productive environment. Even if the therapy occurs in the context of a prison or similar establishment, the room in which therapy takes place should be, conceptually if not in fact, 'outside' the institution, preferably with no visible bars on the windows and offering a comfortable and pleasant physical environment.

In some situations, especially in the prison population, high numbers of prospective clients suffer from mental illnesses and personality disorders that may compromise their suitability for engaging in group therapy, although such may be able to attend group therapy following a period of individual therapy and/or receipt of medical or other treatment for an underlying psychiatric problem. As always, the screening interview is key in determining an appropriate therapeutic strategy. On the other hand, group therapy can be experienced as less anxiety-causing for some, and many such clients benefit enormously from participation.

Above all, the therapist must remember at all times that involuntary clients, just like all other clients, will experience unmet relational needs and their associated emotions as we have laid out in their narratives' 'universal themes' and will respond when they understand that the emotions behind their maladaptive behaviour are not weird and wrong, but normal and understandable.

9
Family and couple work the Needs ABC way

THE NEEDS ABC model, focused as it is on identifying underlying emotions and themes that are easy for everyone to recognise and understand, is ideally suited for application to couples and family therapy, as it is for group therapy, although clearly these bring their own specific challenges to therapy. Furthermore, all of the basic concepts of Needs ABC groupwork are also applicable to individual, couple, and family work, such as making interventive statements as observations and maintaining a focus on emotionally determined process themes. All of the ground we have covered thus far is therefore applicable to individual, family and couples therapy. We will not be providing a full discussion of the application of the Needs ABC model in family and couple work, but some indications of how its tenets can be applied in these contexts.

As in the case of any application of the Needs ABC, the central message that clients must take home from therapy is that they already have the power to change their maladaptive behaviour, just as soon as they have become able to understand the unmet needs that lie behind it. Needs ABC is about realising skills that are already within one's grasp.

In some respects, family therapy resembles 'ordinary' group therapy, insofar as typically there are several individuals in the room, each bringing his or her unique experience to the group. Although any group, even one as inchoate and temporary as a queue in a supermarket, develops its own cultural norms, never are the internal mechanisms as complex as they are in a family. Tolstoy famously said, 'Happy families are all alike; every unhappy family is unhappy in its own way.'[40] This is a simple truth that every family therapist will recognise. Happy families invariably are composed of individuals who, by and large (there being no such thing as a 'perfect' family), respect each other's needs and boundaries, and communicate with the minimum of game-playing. Unhappy families can be maelstroms of unmet needs and maladaptive behaviours, be they acquired from the family of origin or otherwise. The family represents society in microcosm, and is where individual unmet needs, fears and hostilities are played out on a particularly intense scale. In a group of strangers, like the typical therapeutic group, emotive issues can be discussed without fear of future repercussions. In a family, everything is personal. But a family is also like an organism and when one of its members – or one of the organism's components, to continue with our metaphor – is behaving in a malfunctioning way, the ramifications impact on each and every family member and, if left unchecked, will have a ripple effect that will permeate through the lives of those family members and their descendents for generations. This is why, when the dynamics within a family have ceased to function in a healthy manner, therapy can be a good idea. Social workers are horribly familiar with 'problem families' whose problems seem to be passed from parent to child ad infinitum. Children learn from their parents how to behave as adults, and when their parents display maladaptive behaviours, these are what the child inevitably learns as default reactions to stressors in their daily lives. But even families that appear, on the surface, to 'have it all' can develop maladaptive dynamics when relational needs are not being appropriately met, which threaten the emotional wellness and often even the physical integrity of all members.

In any family, parents may tend to act out around unresolved emotional and relational needs from their own childhoods, model their inappropriate problem-solving behaviour – their own childhood survival skills – and often recreate the dysfunctional part of family in which they grew up, even if they attempt to do the exact opposite.

In the case of couples, the contrast between the individuals' desires and the reality that they live every day, together with the mate that they have chosen, can cause terrible problems. The urge to have things done their way – or be in control of their environment – is an overriding instinct in the majority of human beings, and monogamy, or at least serial monogamy, is by far the most common type of marriage or serious relationship in the vast majority of human cultures. Consequently, when problems present in the context of a marriage or serious monogamous relationship, the result is generally profound emotional stress. Greenburg and Johnson cite Bakan when they summarise as follows:

Marriage, along with other forms of coupling, is a social framework for the attainment of adult intimacy; it is also one of the most acceptable social vehicles for human closeness. Just as baby monkeys and children only feel free to venture forth when they can return to the soothing softness of a caretaker, so do adults fare much better in the wide world when they can return to the haven of a supportive marriage.[41]

It is worth mentioning here that couples therapy is applicable to all couples, not just the traditional model of a married heterosexual couple, with or without offspring. Unmarried heterosexual and same-sex couples in long term relations present with problems that do not differ substantially in any way. A couple is a couple is a couple. In each and every case, it is important for the therapist to obtain background information about the family of origin, because relational needs with respect to parents generally seem to develop in the latency period/elementary school phase, and these relational needs are brought to bear in adulthood on the relationship with the opposite sex or, in the case of the homosexual couple, same sex partner. Frequently, behaviours modelled to the child by the same-sex parent are imitated in adulthood. It is worth reiterating that in the experience of this author no significant difference to this pattern presents in the case of same-sex couples.

Families and couples come to therapy for a wide range of reasons, from a self-identified failure to 'get on' to deeply entrenched problematic behaviours including incest, violence towards spouses and/or children or substance abuse on the part of one or more parties to the relationship. Like members of group therapy, families and couples can present themselves voluntarily when they have decided that 'enough is enough' (sometimes following a specific crisis) or can be recommended or 'sent' to therapy by social services or another authoritative body. Not infrequently, one spouse or parent proclaims, 'Either we go to therapy to get this thing sorted out for once and for all, or we're through.'

The good news is that many families and couples, like many individuals, can benefit from therapy, and even seriously dysfunctional family or spousal behavior can be brought to an end, terminating a vicious cycle of maladaptive behaviour and setting the scene for the creation of a more healthy family unit now, and in subsequent generations. Children are programmed to love their parents, and in those cases when they are perforce removed from them because leaving is the better of two evils, they invariably miss their abusive parents, even if they themselves can recognise that they could no longer stay together. Clearly, infinitely better than removing children from inadequate or abusive parents is enabling these parents to better care for their families. Rarely is a successful outcome to therapy as satisfying as in these cases. Whether a family or couple presents itself for therapy, is mandated by court or by social services, attends therapy as a single or multiple unit or in the context of group therapy for more than one family at a time, there is hope – even if only one member of a malfunctioning couple attends.

Applying the Needs ABC model to families and couples

It is crucial to remember that the emotions verbally expressed by members of a family or couple are not necessarily the underlying emotions that are at the root of the problematic behaviour. In fact, very often, emotions that are thought to be inappropriate or 'wrong' are never expressed overtly. The facilitator should listen carefully to client narratives so as to identify the universal themes embedded in them, realising that in the context of individuals who know each other so well, these emotions may be expressed in codified ways that are readily understood by those 'on the inside' and can be less accessible to others. This will call for observing and taking note of nonverbal communications, such as gestures, posture, and so forth as well as by taking careful note of the tone of voice that is used in describing issues within the family or couple. For example, try saying the following sentence in different tones of voice; warm, sarcastic, deadpan:

> 'Joan's a really great housewife and mother. She's so thorough. She never does anything wrong. And she's so patient! Nothing is ever too much for her. Oh, no.'

Without changing the wording, this description of Joan could be used in genuine praise, to parody Joan's hyped-up self-image, or to cruelly belittle a woman who is trying and failing to be a successful, happy housewife and mother. Only a percentage of what we mean is conveyed with mere words.

Teenagers are masters of the art of imbuing an apparently innocuous statement with biting sarcasm and malice, but they do not have a monopoly on this sort of behaviour. Our partners in life, parents and children are typically the people we care most about, and they are also the people we demand the most of. When they seem to let us down, or when we seem to be selling them short, this hurts us much more deeply than similar behaviour with respect to a friend or colleague. As always, when we enter a serious relationship or become

A model for group work and other psychotherapies

parents, behaviours and expectations learned in our families of origin are brought to bear in our new relationships, not always with positive results.

Let's explore some practical examples of family and couple work and ways in which the Needs ABC can be used to assist the individuals involved in identifying and meeting their unmet needs.

A couple on the cusp of parenthood presented themselves for therapy with the following account of their situation:

Example: Mary and Paul

Mary (twenty five) and Paul (thirty one) had been dating for about three years and had moved in together about two years ago. Mary had left Paul about four months ago after what she described as 'years of his complaining and pestering about her untidiness at home.' She had met someone at work, finally decided that 'enough was enough' with Paul and left to live with her new boyfriend. Mary and Paul came for therapy after Mary had discovered that she was pregnant with Paul's baby ('it had to be Paul's because I was not with Mel long enough for it to be his') and decided to keep the child and move back in with him. She stated that she had always loved Paul but found it difficult living with his 'tantrums' and 'obsession' about the cleanliness of his home.

'Sure, I could have done more around the house, but his attitude ticked me off. Why should I help him if he is always criticising me and hounding me about stupid little things like leaving my socks on the floor?'

Paul acknowledged that he was a bit of a 'neat freak' but stated that he *'wasn't asking her to jump off a roof or anything, just to keep the place tidy.'* He added that *'he always liked her a lot – maybe even loved her,'* but that there was something about her that made him 'loose his cool.' He wanted to try to make their relationship work for the sake of their baby and because it was *'time that he grew up and considered having the family that he always wanted.'*

Mary was an 'only child' and described her parents as being emotionally distant though dutiful as parents and that she wanted for nothing as a child. She added that she was still trying to get close to them and, in fact, had made some inroads. Mary mentioned that she had always been in trouble at school – mostly for not attending it – and that she had had to finish her high school in a special program for problem children. She stated that she liked the school, despite its reputation, since she received a lot of help and attention there. Paul, also the only child in his family, described his parents as being extremely attentive to him and

> 'the greatest parents you could ever want ... it wasn't like they spoiled me; it's just that they included me in almost everything and often asked my opinion about certain situations, especially as I got older.'

He related that, when he decided to quit high school in grade nine, his parents supported his decision. *'As long as I made a living and enjoyed what I did; that was good enough for them.'* He added that he was really enjoying his job and felt good about his decision to leave school when he did.

As the session progressed, it was suggested to Mary that it seemed that whenever she became upset or angry at not getting what she wanted she would run away from the situation. A smile appeared on her face as she acknowledged that what had been said sounded familiar. Some situations in Mary's past were reviewed (like not going to school) that appeared to be congruent with that pattern, and when it was suggested that she had done the same thing in leaving Paul she giggled and said: 'You know, I never thought of that one.' As well, she agreed that when she became angry with Paul she would 'totally shut down and turn off.' At that point, Paul exclaimed: 'Yeah, no kidding, you turn into the ice woman.' Paul was asked what happened at home when his parents did not pay attention to him and he replied that that had never happened. He did, however, remember his father yelling at his mother once when she seemed to ignore him.

It was clear from Mary and Paul's narratives that the behavioural patterns they were displaying had been acquired in their families of origin. Towards the end of the session, their therapist explained the following to them:

- We tend to use whatever works to solve problems in relationships, especially solutions that seemed to work as a child;

- When adults use behaviours that worked when they were children, these behaviours usually prove to be problematic since as children we tend to act out, rather than verbally express, our needs;

- As adults we tend to want relationships that will give us what we had as children that felt good, or that will give us what we were missing as children that will make us feel good.

The following was also suggested:

That Paul, having been given a lot of attention as a child in his important relationships (especially by his mother), became frightened when he felt invisible, or marginalised, by Mary. Paul had felt very loved by his parents and associated love with being given a great deal of attention. He acted out his fear of marginalisation stereotypically as anger, once modelled by his father, which only made Mary feel emotionally distanced, or disconnected, from him;

That Mary's worst fear was to feel as emotionally disconnected, or abandoned, by the ones she wanted to be close to as she had been in her family of origin with her parents. Because of her experience of feeling powerless to change things for the better as a child, since her angry acting-out behaviour only proved to get her into more trouble, she tended to run from her anger at Paul for recreating that feeling by turning off, or literally 'running away' by having an affair, since running away seemed to have been her best option as a child.

It was further suggested that Paul's challenge was to 'do nothing' when he became angry so that he could think about how to problem-solve better when he had cooled off, and Mary's was to 'stay put' until she could figure out something better and more empowering as well.

Overall, Mary became frustrated and angry when her need for emotional reliability was not being met (themes: 'abandonment,' intimacy'). Paul seemed to panic when he felt discounted or ignored (theme: 'respect'). Each of them needed to find a way, as adults, to express appropriately when that need was not being met rather than to act out their concerns as children would normally do. It is often easier to rationalise a child's behaviour since they are, indeed, in a position of powerlessness (the adults have the power) and limited responsibility. As an adult, one must take the responsibility to use mature problem-solving strategies since we can use this adult power for better or for worse.

In order to help the couple 'grow up' and into a new relationship, behavioural strategies such as 'mutual time-outs' were gradually introduced into the therapy. The term 'mutual time-out was coined by this author to describe a strategy designed to help the couple deal with any concerns about safety that either has. In the case of the partner whose behaviour poses a threat, it is still incumbent upon him or her to remove his/herself from the scene when the sign is given. For example, since Paul had to learn how to contain his anger when he became fearful that Mary was emotionally distancing herself from him, the couple and the therapist examined whether he could try to catch himself (take a 'time-out') as he began to feel upset and encouraged him to log both his successful and unsuccessful attempts at doing so. In subsequent meetings, both Paul and Mary agreed that he was doing better but Paul stated his concern that there were times that he felt Mary was 'over-reacting' and that she seemed to 'turn off' even when he wasn't feeling angry at all. It was then suggested that Mary give Paul a sign to take a time-out when she started feeling concerned that he would 'lose it.' The therapist explained that, for now, it would give Mary more of a sense of being in control of her safety and that it would make it easier for her not to 'abandon' Paul. This way, Mary's issuing of a time-out serves as a metaphor for being able to keep herself safe regardless of what is going on, allowing her to develop trust in Paul to do whatever it takes to make sure she can feel relationally safe when she feels the need, or when she feels her safety is in jeopardy. Paul agreed to try and later reported that, not only did they both seem to feel closer through their collaborative efforts, but they were also able to sit down and discuss each difficult situation at a mutually accepted time to examine how to better deal with the issue at hand in the future.

Initially, the couple seemed to struggle somewhat with the challenges at hand, but they were able to talk about their failures, as well as their success, in their sessions. In this way, they were able to further fine-tune their strategies. After about the eighth session, they both reported less friction and more success in their collaborative efforts to interrupt their dysfunctional cycle. They stated that understanding their needs as individuals helped them to take things less personally and react accordingly. Paul seemed to understand how hurtful and frustrating his yelling was and was able, on several occasions when he 'still lost it,' to apologise in a more meaningful way. Mary was also more empathic about 'shutting out Paul' but also seemed extremely motivated to change her behaviour because she felt it was 'silly and childish' and was something she did not want to do when she became a mother.

At this point, Mary and Paul were able to cut back their sessions from once weekly to twice monthly, and then to once every three to four weeks. After about six months, they decided to come in when they needed to for a 'refresher,' but only came in twice in the next twelve months. They therapist recently received an e-mail telling him that all was going well but with their child now being a year old that they might need to come in again sometime for some help. He has not heard from them since.

In our second example, we have the opportunity to meet a couple that, despite their problems as the heads of a growing family, is giving their family unit the opportunity to escape from the dysfunctional patterns that marked both childhoods:

Example: Chris and Erin

Chris (thirty four) and Erin (thirty two) have been married for ten years. They have three children (Jacob, eight, Steven, seven and Jillian, four and a half). Chris and Erin came into therapy describing that they were in a state of crisis and that Erin was considering leaving the relationship because of Chris's controlling and emotionally abusive behaviour. Chris admitted that he was controlling and that he 'had to have a say in everything that she did.' He also admitted that he was jealous and untrusting in general and, even though he loved Erin very much, always felt somewhat distrustful of her motives and loyalty. He stated that he had agreed to come in for help when he discovered that she had 'stolen' the money he had put aside for her for emergencies and that, because they had not had sex for almost six months, he was worried she was having an affair; 'What else would she need that money for?'

Erin immediately piped in, saying that it would be almost impossible for her to have an affair because he was always either with her or calling her. She stated that she had taken the money because she was tired of being 'told off' every time she needed money for 'a bottle of shampoo.' She said that she was generally tired of his criticisms and directive and that, in a sense, she had 'given up,' because 'if Chris refuses to trust me, why should I even bother?'

Erin, the youngest of six, grew up in a family in which her father drank and abused her mother and her two older brothers. She stated that 'when the shit began to hit the fan' she would run over to her girlfriend's house. She said that she had not spoken to her father since she left home at the age of sixteen, and would not have spoken to him unless she had to, even then, for fear he would 'beat the crap out of me too.' She said that the only person that she ever felt close to was her mother, and that they were even closer since her father died about six years ago of cirrhosis of the liver. 'And good riddance to him, too.'

Chris described his parents as extremely critical and 'selfish.' 'Everything had to be on their terms,' he declared. 'I also left home at eighteen to get away from their constant nagging and complaining about whatever I did.' He went on to complain that his mother was 'never really interested in being a mother,' because 'she was always busy doing everything but being with me or my younger brother.' Chris went on to describe that their financial situation had been extremely tight after his business went under and that, even though he was optimistic about the future of his present business venture, 'stealing the money was like sticking in the knife and turning it as well.'

The therapist suggested to the couple that what had inadvertently happened is that, as so often happens despite the best of intentions, they each had recreated their worst nightmares from their families of origin. Chris had become as violent and controlling as Erin's father had and Erin had become Chris's mother with regard to her aloofness (emotional distancing) when he became upset. Erin agreed that when she felt Chris was attacking her she would become 'as cold as ice' and Chris also agreed that he became very upset when he felt her pulling away from him, and that he felt inadequate as a husband, especially because of the bankruptcy. The therapist and couple continued discussing their relationship, past and present. Describing their emotional needs to them, the therapist suggested that competency was a 'huge button' for Chris; that his anger actually represented his fear that he could not measure up and that his 'jealousy' was about feeling that, because he was not 'good enough,' Erin would go elsewhere. As we have pointed out before, men frequently use terms such as 'anger' to vocalise underlying emotions that would be more productively described using words such as 'fear' or 'anxiety.'

Erin's need, on the other hand, was to have emotional reliability from her spouse as opposed to the emotional abandonment that she had experienced as a child at the hands of her alcoholic father. Chris's 'triggers' were around competency. In fact, Erin stated that when they first met she had 'tested' Chris by trying to provoke him into violence but that he never made her feel unsafe. Chris admitted that Erin had looked up to him and now it seemed that, no matter what he did, he always 'screwed it up with her.' Chris emphatically stated that he did not want to lose Erin and would do whatever he could to regain her trust.

The therapist asked the couple to consider the following plan of action: Even though they both had behaviours that could be improved upon, it would be difficult for Erin to change her behaviour in light of the violent nature of Chris's behaviour toward her. The therapist asked Chris to consider that he would have to take the first step in showing Erin that she could, once again, be safe with him, even when he was upset. He agreed and some behavioural tactics such as 'time out' and logging were offered and the couple was encouraged to see how it would go between this and their next session. When the therapist suggested that, eventually, Erin would have to consider not giving Chris the 'cold shoulder,' she shook her head saying that she was not prepared to do too much until Chris 'did his part'; then she would see what she could do.

Before the session ended, the therapist asked how they felt the session went. Both agreed that in understanding what their relational needs were they would be able to consider ways of communicating when they were not being met. Chris confided that he had never considered how powerful his aggressive behaviour was, especially considering Erin's problems growing up. Erin was thankful that she understood his powerful reaction to her behaviour considering his financial problems, but reasserted that she was not prepared to look at her part in this until he could regain her trust.

Combining group and couple work

There are times when couples will benefit both from attending group therapy (separately or together) and couple work, concomitantly or subsequently. Group therapy gives people the opportunity to explore their emotional geography in an environment away from their family or life partner, and thus without the recrimination and emotionally loaded scenarios that these situations can lead to. With a better understanding of their own emotional needs and triggers, the individuals in question may present for family or group therapy better able to deal with the issues that arise.

The following case study refers to an older couple that presented for couple work following having made some progress separately in their respective groups.

Example: Sybil and Sam

Sybil (58) and Sam (63), who have lived in Montreal all their lives, have been married for 34 years. They have three adult children who have moved away, and are the grandparents of three grandchildren (two from Todd, 33, who lives in Alberta, and one from Nancy, 29, who lives in Toronto). They have been working together ever since they decided to have children. They both had agreed that, since Sam was self-employed in advertising, Sybil could work from home, taking care of all the bookkeeping, etc. while Sam could travel to promote his services. Previously, Sybil worked as a legal secretary and did accounting on the side, while Sam had employed the services of an elderly woman who was in failing health and was hoping to retire.

Sybil and Sam had hoped that, when Nancy finally left home, Sam would not have to work so much, making it possible for them to travel: 'We have always dreamed of seeing the pyramids in Egypt, but we've never had the time to get away.' However, without warning, about a year after Nancy left, Sam had a fairly serious heart attack. He recovered and was told that if he took care of himself he could lead a normal life and return to his usual routine, although he would have to watch his diet and carry 'nitro' tablets with him, 'just in case of a problem.' He has not had any problems for the past four years and feels 'fit as a fiddle,' according to himself. He has, however, stopped doing his light exercises and swimming. Sybil has added volunteer work to her list of things to do twice weekly and continues to swim (without Sam) four or five times per week.

About two months before applying to the domestic violence clinic, Sam described an incident of violence in which he had slapped Sybil quite soundly across the face after she had, according to him, spilled hot coffee on him. She had phoned the police and charges were placed that were later dropped. She told him that if she was going to stay with him he would have to go for help. Apparently what had happened (according to Sybil who was later contacted by and offered services in a women's support group) was that she had bolted from the room in disgust after Sam had called her a name during one of their frequent shouting matches. Unfortunately, she had been holding a cup of coffee in her hand which spilled out onto Sam. Sam had apparently screamed and 'slugged' her. She had been so taken aback that she dialled 911. It was normal for them to have a 'spat' from time to time, she had reported, but things seemed to have gotten worse since his heart attack. She admitted that she often felt that he might strike her sooner or later.

On being asked to talk a little about her background, Sybil described herself as having been extremely independent since the age of ten. Her father had been hit by a car and could not work as he was bound to a wheelchair. Her mother had to go out to work, leaving Sybil behind to care for her dad as well as her younger sister and brother. She left home as soon as she could ('couldn't wait') and was gainfully employed and financially independent until she became pregnant.

A model for group work and other psychotherapies

Sam was the third youngest of four children. He had an older sister, an older brother and a younger sister. He stated that he had always been very close to his mother, who died about two years ago (his father passed away about ten years ago). He implied that he was her favourite and that he could 'do no wrong' so far as she was concerned. He had lived with his mother until he met Sybil, and continued to feel close to his mother 'until the end.' In the early years of their marriage, he was not at home much but did spend quality time with the family when he could. Both agreed that they had a good relationship in the early years and validated each other as parents. Sybil felt that he could not have done too much around the house at that time since 'things weren't easy then and it was hard to make a living.'

Sam spent ten weeks in the men's group at the domestic violence clinic and appeared to have difficulty taking responsibility for his treatment. Sam continuously reported during the group sign-in that things had been going better since he made his decision to come to the group and that nothing had changed from week to week: 'Everything is great.' Sybil did some individual work as well as engaging in the women's group for an eight week session. She stated that she did not feel afraid of Sam at this point, although she was a little confused about what she wanted to do about the relationship.

After attending ten of fifteen required sessions in a domestic violence treatment group (Sybil had been attending the women's support group during this time) a decision was made in collaboration with Sybil and Sam to engage in couple work. Sybil felt it was safe to do so and Sam said 'sounds O.K. to me' (although he did not seem convinced). They engaged in twelve weeks of couple treatment. Sybil's group had already terminated and Sam stayed in the men's group only until he had completed the suggested fifteen weeks.

In the above example, it would first be important to examine what each client should work on in their group work treatments. From the couple's recent history, it seems that Sam sees himself as a bit of a 'victim' with 'abandonment' being his Achilles heel (the violence having occurred when Sybil tried to leave during an argument), while Sybil appears to need to do more in times of adversity (when things seem to be out of control) and 'competency' in keeping things 'on track' appears to be something she needs to feel for herself. These issues seem to be corroborated in the developmental histories they related, and in the description given by the group workers of their participation in their group therapies. The message embedded in Sam's narrative seems to say: 'I can't do this alone,' while Sybil indicates the opposite by stating: 'Independence is important since you can't always count on others.' Her inability to get Sam's attention appears to be extremely frustrating since, without it, she cannot 'fix' him. Sam appears to indicate that she has abandoned him emotionally at a critical time by not understanding how frightening his medical problem has been for him and that he needs help and support to move forward – that he can't 'just do it.'

In their respective groups, the therapeutic task would be to help Sam and Sybil to recognise what is missing from their relationship (their needs-deficit) as well as to examine some possibilities for coming closer by getting these needs met. Since they were also able to engage in couple work, and therefore have had the opportunity to work collaboratively as a couple, the couple counsellor could reaffirm that these relational needs were accurate by 'checking them out' with each of them and help them to understand how to communicate these needs in a productive manner and how to 'stay on top' of their relationship by being sensitive to the other's interpersonal expectations. Needless to say, if group therapy had been the only option, then role-plays, reaching for feelings and other exercises could have been utilised to help them to improve their communication skills and share their relational needs. By working with the couple, the therapist can create a more 'in vivo' experience while fine-tuning both the needs-getting and the needs-giving strategies that are most productive for the couple as an entity.

Family therapy

Because a family deals with individuals of different ages and with different abilities to express themselves, as well as structures of authority and power unique to the family in question, the facilitator must be able to adapt his or her style of applying the Needs ABC model to the particular circumstances at hand. Let's explore an example:

Example: The Murphy family

The Murphy family has been recommended to attend therapy because of ongoing problems that recently reached a head when their eldest child, Tony, was found to be taking ecstasy tablets at school. Tony, who is sixteen years old, has four younger siblings, Joanna (thirteen), Mark (eleven), Susan (seven) and Alex (two). The Murphy family has been known to social services for some time, because of an episode a few years ago when Pete, the father, spent some time in jail after he was apprehended stealing money from envelopes at the post office where he worked.

Pete willingly admits that he has a problem with alcohol, and says that he 'Would like to stop drinking,' but that he doesn't know how. His wife and the children's mother, Gloria, also drinks heavily but says that 'it's not a problem because when I am drunk I just fall asleep, not like Pete who starts shouting and behaving obnoxiously.' The couple have had their arguments, but feel that they have a strong marriage.

Although things are clearly not ideal in the Murphy household, the four children are well-nourished and cared for, attend school regularly and in the case of the three older ones, display academic performances average and above average for their age, although all three are known to be unruly when they do not get their way.

However, when Tony was found in high school with a number of ecstasy tablets on his person, the underlying dysfunctionality of the way in which the family members relate to each other was revealed. Tony, hitherto a rather bright and high-achieving teenager, was expelled from his school and, so far, has refused to start in another school so that he can complete his high school education. Pete had always been a rowdy drunk, never a violent one, but when Tony was expelled, he 'went on a tear,' coming home to roust his son from bed and beat him up while the children's mother screamed in horror and the three younger children watched, terrified. Tony fled the house and was missing for almost two weeks, before turning up the worse for wear after having spent the last while, 'hanging with my friends and smoking dope – they understand me, even if my parents don't' as he put it.

As a result of the stress affecting the household, both parents have been drinking too much; even more than usual. Pete had found work as a labourer, but he lost it because he kept turning up late, and Gloria, who is a housewife, has been neglecting her responsibility to make sure that her children arrive in school clean and on time.

Because the parents have a long history of taking good care of their children, despite their personal difficulties, social services is very reluctant to take the children into care. The Murphies have been told that, if they want to keep their family together, they will have to attend family therapy. Both parents have also been strongly encouraged to attend AA to try and get their drinking under control.

The therapy sessions are attended by the whole family, save the youngest child. The therapist notes that both parents seem strongly motivated and, up to now, the sessions have been going well. Pete and Gloria are attending AA, although neither of them has yet managed to stop drinking.

Discussing his family of origin, Pete says that his father, a miner, was a very heavy drinker and died young of cirrhosis of the liver. His mother was 'a saint' and had to work to support her seven children, most of whom went on to finish high school. However, she was so busy that she had little time to do anything other than make sure that the children were fed and clothed and that the house was reasonably clean. Overall, Pete described a situation whereby emotional reliability from his parents was elusive at best. Gloria grew up in a more affluent home. Her parents had just three children, and her father was a skilled worker in a factory, earning enough to support her mother's work in the home. Gloria stated that she came from an extremely close-knit family, in which the parents' primary focus was on the children and the family's wellbeing.

Pete and Gloria agree that Pete tends to drink when he is stressed. Since he was caught stealing ('It was the most stupid thing I've ever done. I was drunk at the time and I really regret throwing away all these years of experience'), Pete has felt stressed 'most of the time,' he says. He had worked very hard at the post office, and had been 'set up for life in a pensionable job' until he did 'one stupid thing' that destroyed his plans.

Gloria says she started drinking 'to keep Pete company' and that she is reasonably confident that she can stop, but that she thinks it would be easier when things have calmed down.

In conversation with the children, the therapist quickly reveals that they have experienced emotions of embarrassment and shame associated with their father's legal troubles, and that they feel rejected by their parents' behaviour: 'Mom and Dad just sit there drinking beer and they completely ignore us!' Tony is the most difficult to engage with, as it seems that he feels that he is responsible for getting the whole family 'into trouble' and that, from now on, he is going to be scapegoated as the one who 'screwed the whole thing up.'

It seems quite apparent even from the early sessions of therapy that, in becoming involved in using to deal with his anxiety, Tony is following his father's example. All Tony's life, Pete has responded to feelings of powerlessness and/or fear of abandonment by 'drugging himself' with alcohol. At first, Pete is reluctant to accept this analysis of the situation, saying: 'Yeah, but I just drink beer. Everyone drinks beer – even the president! Drugs are a completely different kettle of fish.' However, when it is pointed out to him by Gloria that Tony's behaviour is identical to his father's, regardless of the purpose or the intoxicating substance in question, Pete concedes the point.

As the sessions continue, the Murphy family and the therapist work together to find a feasible solution to the situation facing the whole family. It is clear that a pattern of fears of powerlessness and abandonment, as well as concerns about their respective competencies, runs through much of the family's interactions both within the family group and with other significant relationships each individual faces, at school, at work or with friends. Pete, for example, thought that he would not be loved if he let down the family financially, having historical concerns about emotional reliability. Although there is also a lot of affection within the family, the fact that the parents are frequently effectively 'absent' because they have been drinking threatens to perpetuate a behavioural pattern that is already there. As well, Pete's (albeit drunken) criticism of his family because of his felt incompetence has produced an anxiety about either 'measuring up' or being punished. While it would be advisable for Pete and Gloria to continue attending AA, it is also important that the family spend more 'good' time together. Because of Pete's drinking, Gloria has felt a sense of betrayal since Pete seems to choose 'the bottle' over her (and the family). While they are all busy with their own obligations, it is agreed that they will all spend at least two hours together in evening 'with the television turned off' so that they can eat together and talk through the events of the day.

For now, Tony is strongly resistant to returning to school, where he feels that he will be 'picked on' because he has already been marked as a trouble-maker. This has been exacerbated by his father's criticism which has given him the impression that he is 'defective' and will not measure up to others' expectations. As an alternative, the therapist suggests that he find work and look for another school to attend next term. Tony does not have much difficulty in obtaining a job in a local music shop. The work is relatively simple and paid at the minimum wage, but he says that it is 'fun' and that he likes listening to music all day and knowing what is popular: 'Who would have thought that listening to hip hop qualified me for a job!' He also says that he is learning a lot and might be given a raise, proving his competency, if he continues to work at the weekends while going to school.

Pete acknowledges that when he is not drinking he is able to see how fortunate he is in having such a fine family that, overall, has done well despite the chaotic home environment. He is encouraged to validate his family's strengths and assets and find ways to show them how important they are to him. One thing Pete decided to do was throw a surprise birthday party for Gloria and worked with all the children in cooking the food and decorating the home. This act of loyalty demonstrated to the family their importance to him. They all gleefully recounted how they enjoyed being with friends and family, how great dad was, and how mom 'didn't have a clue!'

The family attends therapy for a period of ten weeks, during which time considerable improvement in the family dynamic is noted by therapist and family alike.

The following case study refers to an adolescent client, who attended therapy at the prompting of his father because of his difficulties in navigating his family circumstances:

Example: Jeremy

Jeremy is an extremely well-spoken sixteen year old client who had spent about eighteen months in a Juvenile Detention Centre for uttering death threats to a classmate at his school. He and his thirteen year old brother Lionel have been raised predominantly by their father since their mother walked out on them when Jeremy was six years old. She apparently had been heavily involved in drug use and left one day for no apparent reason. His father, Richard, a forty-one year old technician at an auto-parts manufacturing facility, took a second job after his wife left, 'to make more money to be better able to give my kids what they need.' Richard left his sons with their grandmother (his mother), whom Jeremy described as 'an old woman who thought she was in the 'old country.'" The therapist had initially met with Richard who told me about Jeremy's history and that he had been placed on time-release Ritalin since elementary school. He told the therapist that when Jeremy got to high school he began his acting-out, which included refusing to take his medication. He had been compliant since being placed, and it seemed that the medication did help somewhat with Jeremy's impulsivity.

When Jeremy came in he appeared angry, stating, 'Let's get this over with so I can spend some time with my father.' Needless to say, the therapist used lots of empathy with how he felt, allying with how he must feel about being sent away despite the fact that his threats to his classmates were a serious matter. Jeremy was able to tell the therapist about how his mother played almost no part in his life and (somewhat tearfully) how much he wanted to be with his father and brother. He related how his mother never seemed to have time for anyone and was either 'stoned' or 'missing in action' as he described it. He seemed constantly close to tears when he discussed his relationship with his younger brother and how his father always tried to get them the things they wanted. As the meeting progressed, the therapist suggested to Jeremy that family was very important to him and that he probably missed his father now, like he did when he was with his grandmother. At this point Jeremy burst into tears and, after he had calmed himself, the therapist said: 'It must feel awful to feel so unimportant that your father would get a second job and leave you with your grandmother instead of spending time with you and your brother.' Jeremy looked up wide eyed, thought for a moment and said: 'Yeah, and I'm glad he only has one job now!'

By continuing to ally with the feelings that caused Jeremy's behaviour, rather than examining his behaviour per se, Jeremy was able to cautiously engage in a conversation with the therapist that eventually exposed his relational needs. It was apparent that he felt abandoned by those he loved and also marginalised, and that his perception was that he was inherently defective. He admitted that since no one cared enough to spend time with him that he must be 'bad.'

'Who cares what I do?' he said. 'I might as well live up to what they have already decided about me.' The good news was that his father was prepared to do whatever it took to be with his children as much as possible and had quit his second job just before Jeremy was referred to therapy by child protection services. Jeremy was obviously happy about this and said that Lionel was as well. (In fact, Richard had told the therapist in a previous meeting that Lionel was doing better at school and at home now that he was around him more.) As Jeremy and the therapist ended their session, they agreed to meet as a family (Richard, Lionel and Jeremy) to talk together about what would make them all happier so that everyone could be heard.

Another boy (Roger), this time pre-adolescent, was brought to therapy by his mother (Andrea) after she had contacted a therapist with regard to her concern about Roger's violent acting-out behaviour. Andrea stated that her son used profanity in an abusive manner towards her and 'the final straw' and precipitating factor for the phone call to the therapist was when they were having one of their apparently regular arguments and Roger had 'come at her' with a hammer. ('He looked like he was possessed or something.')

Andrea had contacted a crisis centre and was given the name of a therapist as well as advice to call the police. Subsequently, a friend of hers gave her the name of a therapist whom she knew. Andrea opted to come in and see the therapist her friend suggested rather than call the police since she was concerned about the ramifications of getting the law involved:

Example: Andrea

Andrea, a 37-year-old professional, had been married to Roger's father for six years. They had separated when Roger (now twelve) was four. Andrea stated that her 'ex' had been both physically and verbally abusive towards her, and that she was concerned that Roger was mimicking his father's behaviour. She added that her estranged husband continued to avoid both alimony payments and child support, although he did agree to collaborate around visitation.

The therapist first met with both Roger and his mother and was informed that his mother had originally left Roger with his father to move far enough away so that she would not be pursued and further abused. She had returned and moved into her own apartment about six months later when she felt that it was safe to do so and 'took Roger back' to live with her. Andrea went on to explain (while looking directly at Roger) that he was spoiled and only did what she asked if she bribed him with money or promised to buy him something he wanted.

After meeting with both together for about fifteen minutes, the therapist was able to convince Roger to meet with him alone by suggesting that he might want to discuss some things that he did not want to talk about in front of his mother.

Roger admitted to sometimes slapping himself in the face or calling himself names, especially when he tried to do something (e.g. build a Lego model) and had difficulty or failed. He seemed very forthcoming but appeared to have difficulty with topics that were shame-based (e.g. taking out a hammer just to get his mother's attention and, as a result, scaring her badly). In addition, he appeared to understand that his behaviour was inappropriate but stated that, at times, he could not control himself.

A model for group work and other psychotherapies

When Andrea rejoined the session to arrange for future work together, the therapist made a point of giving Roger some say in the matter of whether he would like to return to 'discuss some more stuff' or not. Roger agreed to come back in two weeks and to try to remember when he was 'bad' and when he was 'good' in the meantime. He also said he did not want to go to day-camp because his friend would not be there, but finally agreed after a bribe from his mother. As they were leaving his mother began to remind him of some of his past digressions, despite the therapist's efforts to contain her. At that point, Roger ran out saying, 'I'm not coming here anymore.'

It was quite clear that Roger's internal testimony went something like this:

'I am 'bad' because I am not good enough. I am not good enough because I mess up when I try to do something; people don't want to be with anybody who messes up the way I do; I only get people's attention when I get mad but then I feel bad about what I do and that makes me madder. Money (concrete objects vs. emotional reliability) is the only thing I can count on, so I want the people I love to show that they love me too by giving me money.'

Rogers unmet emotional needs clearly centred around feeling defective or incompetent and his difficulty in controlling his relational environment to any extent. For her part, Andrea's testimony ran along the lines of:

'He reminds me of his father who betrayed me. I am furious at his father for manipulating me. I punish my son for his father's mistakes.'

The bitter irony, of course, is that Andrea's reactions to her son's violent behaviour (betrayal), her inability to control him, and feeling disrespected as a mother as a result, are helping to create an adult whose unmet emotional needs practically guarantee perpetuating the dysfunctional behavioural patterns that have damaged his family. Unless Roger's need to feel adequate (competent and emotionally connected) can be identified and appropriately met now, while he is still a child, he will continue his quest for competency and emotional safety as an adult using the same tactics he is employing as a child.

Overall, it appears that both Roger and his mother are behaviourally saying: 'if you really loved me you would understand what I need by doing what I want.' If Roger returns to therapy, he and the therapist will examine his needs in this important relationship with regard to appropriate parent-child dynamics and hierarchy, help his mother not to 'confuse' her son with his father, support Roger's competencies, and reinforce their emotional connection to each other. They can also examine better ways for Roger to get his mother's attention without being so 'scary.'

Use of role play

Role play can be an extremely powerful tool in any form of psychotherapy, and so it is in the context of family and couples therapy. In such units, relationships can be so complex and fraught that individuals can find themselves never fully able to express what they are feeling without falling into well-worn grooves of miscommunication and blame. By stepping away from their usual roles, and trying to imagine how the world looks from another's point of view, much can be achieved. Let's look at an example:

Example: Paul and John

Paul and John have been together for eight years in a stable, committed relationship. John has no children, but Paul has a teenaged son from an earlier marriage. The separation was quite amicable, his former wife is happily remarried and, although his son, William, lives primarily with his mother, Paul continues to have an active role in his upbringing. Paul and his former wife, Michelle, signed joint-custody papers and have consistently honoured their agreement. William spends at least every second weekend and much of his vacation time with his father. Latterly, however, he has been behaving in an increasingly disruptive way in his father's house, and his behaviour seems to be directed primarily towards John. This in turn has been causing considerable tension between John and Paul. John feels that Paul should 'control' his son (apparently feeling marginalised by Paul with regard to William's attitude towards him) while Paul feels that John is being insensitive and narrow-minded by not supporting his expertise as a parent.

'When William was little everything was fine between us,' John says. 'But William is fifteen now, and he is getting really obnoxious. I used to be his buddy, but now he has no respect. He breaks my stuff, talks back and generally just tries to get on my nerves. And Paul doesn't do anything to control him. It's my home too. The other day I found him poking through my personal things yet again. It's just getting to be way too much.'

Paul is clearly exasperated by what John narrates, and responds to his feeling that William wants his father's loyalty by saying in an angry tone: 'John doesn't get it. William is my responsibility. He's my son, and I love him. Why should I do anything to make him feel less than welcome in our home? It's already difficult for him, having a Dad who is openly gay. He's dealt with that really well. There's no way I'm going to do anything to make him feel that he's not welcome. John doesn't have any children. He doesn't understand and, to be frank, I don't see any sign that he's even making an effort. He doesn't seem to recognise that William is just a kid. He can't be held responsible the same way as an adult.'

'I wonder how you would like it if someone broke your oh-so-precious vintage record collection,' John retorted.

Before things get out of hand, the therapist intervenes with the suggestion that it might be worth trying to see things from the other's point of view, and invites Paul and John to change roles for a few minutes. After some initial awkwardness, John and Paul manage to 'get into their roles' quite well.

Speaking as Paul, John says: 'I suppose it would be easier if maybe you cleared off a bit at weekends and did your own thing so that I could concentrate on my kid (implying that respect – in this case, for Paul's relationship with his son – is an important relational need for him). I guess now that he's a teenager he needs a dad's input more than ever. I think he's jealous of you. That's probably why he's been so invasive of your space.'

Speaking for John, Paul says: 'I guess you know best since he is your son' (supporting his own need to feel acknowledged for his competency as a parent).

John nods approvingly at which point Paul, breaking out of his role exclaims: 'Now we're getting there!'

The couple agreed that John would try to 'make himself scarce' a bit more at weekends, so that Paul and William can spend more time together as father and son. In this way John can have some free time, relieving some tension without feeling he is abandoning Paul, and can also expect more positive attention (respect) when William is not there since the animosity that Paul had developed will be diminished, permitting him to both parent and limit-set more appropriately with his son. John's acceptance of this plan supports Paul's adequacy as a parent. William will not feel the need to compete with John and will be able to accept his father's limits more readily.

This approach resulted in a much improved situation at home and, quite quickly, between John and William, too.

In this case, the couple's problem centred around a relatively straightforward practical issue – William's need to feel his father's loyalty despite the fact that he no longer lives with William's mother, and John's need to be respected with regard to his position in the household by Paul. In this case, resorting to role play enabled both John and Paul to break out of the loop of failed communications by projecting their needs onto their personas in their roles and to find a workable solution by better understanding their relational needs.

Therapist self-disclosure

Therapist self-disclosure can be a powerful tool in family and couples therapy, just as it can in group therapy. As well as demonstrating that she does not see herself as 'above it all' but has experienced her own issues and problems in the context of her relationships and family, the therapist is in an excellent position to model appropriate self-disclosure in the therapeutic context. Let's look at an example, in the context of family therapy:

Example: Ahmed and Sonya

Ahmed and Sonya have been married for fifteen years, and have three children. The couple is affluent and the family lacks for nothing materially but as their children have grown older, the parents have developed very different parenting styles, which have been confusing the children and leading to a considerable degree of stress in the home, especially as their two oldest, Yasmin and John (they are twins), have reached adolescence. Ahmed believes that the children should devote themselves to their school work and socialise very little, reasoning that 'there will be plenty of time for that when they are older and established in their careers.' Sonya, on the other hand, does not think that her children 'need to be bookworms' and says that although she wants them to do well at school, she also feels that it is important for them to socialise and see their friends: 'Otherwise, how are they going to learn how to be members of society?' The parents have reached a situation in which they often disagree about how their adolescent offspring should behave, give them conflicting directions and sometimes, especially in Ahmed's case, punish them for actions that were permitted by the other parent. This in turn is leading to disagreement and strife between the couple and a general atmosphere of disquiet in the home.

The family came for therapy after Ahmed and Sonya returned from a night out and found the twins rather the worse for wear after having polished off almost four bottles of wine. The scene developed into a shouting match during which Ahmed blamed Sonya for being too lenient, Sonya yelled at Ahmed that the kids were rebelling because he was 'repressing' them and the twins burst into drunken sobs.

Fortunately, the family decided to arrange to begin therapy the following day, before the situation escalated.

During the family's intake interview, the therapist determined that Ahmed, who was from Pakistan originally, had come from a poor but ambitious family and had 'worked every hour that God sent him' to graduate high school and get a scholarship to attend medical school in Lahore. He was now a paediatrician at a major public hospital and often worked 80 hour weeks. Ahmed had no doubts about his competency, but 'respect' appeared to be a considerable relational need. He was, in fact, very respected in his position, and enjoyed his work and the respect it afforded him. Sonya worked as a physiotherapist at the same hospital – part time since the twins were born. In fact, this is where they had originally met. Sonya had been born into an upper middle class family in Ontario. Her parents had run a food wholesale outlet, had been able to support her through university and had helped the couple purchase their first home. Sonya seemed to feel that she was very competent, but Ahmed seemed to undermine these feelings, especially when it came to parenting the children.

It was not difficult to see that each parent had acquired their parenting style from their family of origin. The therapist suspected that cultural differences might also play a part in the situation currently confronting the family, although this had not been explicitly stated by the parents. Overall she realised that Ahmed was concerned that he was not being given the respect he felt he had 'earned' with regard to his parenting. After all, wasn't he a successful physician who had made good decisions, both in his personal and professional life, meriting the respect due from family, friends and colleagues? Sonya, on the other hand, felt that her competency in making good decisions for her family was being challenged despite the fact she had been able, not only to become a success herself, but also to support her own family in the process. The therapist, in an effective display of self-disclosure to gently illuminate these possibilities, said:

> 'You know, my husband is from Greece and I grew up right here. We never considered that there were any major cultural differences between us, but boy did that change when our son was born! Right from the very first day, I found Spiros really over-protective, just like a typical 'old country' Greek parent combined with 'Father Knows Best.' He wanted to wrap him in swaddling, and I told him that swaddling went out in the Dark Ages. He thought that I was way too careless when I thought I was helping Josh to be independent. I thought 'What's with him? After all, I am a helping professional!' After a while, we figured out a lot of it was due to our different cultural backgrounds and found a compromise, but it took us a while.'

Sonya's initial reaction is to shake her head, but Ahmed butts in with understanding all over his face:

> 'Yes, I think that's a big part of it. In Pakistan, children are supposed to be respectful to their parents, not disobedient. When they don't behave as they should, it's not a small thing! I didn't like to work hard when I was fourteen either, but my parents made sure I did and now I'm a doctor. All I want is the same for my own children.'

'Yeah, I suppose you have a point,' Sonya said. 'My parents belonged to the school of 'they have to learn for themselves'. I learned a lot even before I went to university. It looks like the apple didn't fall far from the tree for either of us!'

'Mind you,' Ahmed added thoughtfully, 'we both turned out O.K., even if our parents took very different approaches with us.'

The twins look at each other in exasperation, and Yasmin says:

> 'I think the two of you need to talk to each other and find a compromise instead of just yelling at us all the time! I know we were stupid to get drunk but it's really hard to be good when we don't know what we are supposed to be doing in the first place!'

As well as helping to facilitate conversation by modelling self-disclosure, the therapist has made it possible for Ahmed, Sonya and their children to stop accusing each other of being unreasonable on an individual level. Instead, the parents especially are now able to discuss their different cultural backgrounds and how these influence their parenting styles. Now the family is able to discuss more productively about how the children's confusion had challenged their competency. For so long as a failure to identify the underlying cause of the problem remained, Sonya had felt marginalised and Ahmed had felt betrayed by the situation that had developed in their home.

Moving on

As stated at the beginning of this book, the desired result of therapy using the Needs ABC model is not to foster a sense of dependence on therapy or on the therapist, but to enable clients to move on with their lives by helping them to reach a point whereby they no longer need therapy at all. In all Needs ABC informed therapies, this is achieved by helping the family or spousal units acquire the tools they need to stop 'being unhappy in their own way.' This usually means that, by the time the client (or therapeutic unit) arrives, they are in 'survival mode' and are using the emotional and relational survival skills they have learned in childhood. By recognising these traits and understanding where they come from, clients can learn to develop new survival skills that function more productively in the context of their re-negotiated family unit.

10
After treatment

ALTHOUGH MANY CLIENTS – those attending group, individual, couple and family therapy alike – will take part in more than one episode of therapy, it should always be borne in mind that the end result of therapy should be its becoming obsolete for its participants. That this is the goal of therapy should be made clear to all clients when they commence therapy and as they progress through it, whether the group is closed or open. Nobody should feel surprised that they are expected to 'work through' their emotions with regard to termination towards the end of leaving therapy.

The Needs ABC approach is dedicated to assisting clients to identify and meet their emotional and relational needs and, if they succeed in doing so, they will no longer feel the urge to engage in the maladaptive behaviour that has been blighting their interpersonal relationships for so long. In other words, they will naturally progress towards the termination of their time in therapy. Although many clients may find more than one period of therapy necessary to reaching their goal, their goal and that of the therapist should be a future in which therapy is no longer necessary.

One might suppose that becoming able to move away from therapy would be a time of celebration, but in fact many people find it enormously difficult to cease attending therapy. Even those who seem to have moved beyond the need for therapy, and who recognise this in themselves can find it very difficult to do so. The group, the family, the individual or the couple's interaction with the therapist, has become a 'safe' place in which taboo emotions, feelings and behaviour can be discussed without fear of retribution, unlike the outside world where one has to constantly monitor one's behaviour and 'edit' what one would like to say. For people who have frequently spent a lifetime repressing the truth about their feelings, letting go of this safe place can be distressing. Facing the world without

Needs ABC: Acquisition and Behaviour Change

the safety valve offered by therapy can seem daunting indeed – and daunting in ways that are different for everybody. In fact, the only safe generalisation one can make about termination, as ending therapy is referred to, is that it is a very different experience for everyone. As Yalom says:

> Some…may achieve a great deal in a few months, whereas others require years of…therapy. Some patients have far more ambitious goals that others do; it would not be an exaggeration to state that some patients, satisfied with their therapy, terminate in approximately the same state in which others begin…[42]

We have already discussed in various contexts the importance the Needs ABC model places on emphasising the emotions and themes behind behaviours rather than behaviours themselves. Our model is built on the fact that finding healthy ways to meet unmet needs to replace maladaptive ways will result in the unhelpful behaviour being eliminated. It is crucial to maintain this focus as clients move towards a phase in their lives in which they will not require therapy, but will instead be prepared to tackle the challenges in their everyday lives with the resources that they have acquired as a result of attending therapy. They need to know that they will still be 'the same person' and that, although they have identified their maladaptive behaviours and the reasons behind them, they do not have to struggle to change their identity or their likes and dislikes. Moving on from therapy is not about being reborn as a different person. It is about being more genuinely the same person, only happier by being better able to accept and deal with unmet needs in a manner that hurts neither themselves nor the people they care about. In some cases, moving beyond therapy can even be about really being oneself for the first time.

As a fixed period in therapy draws to a close, or as a client gradually begins to feel 'ready' to leave open-ended therapy, the facilitator can assist with the process by reminding them of the progress they have made in identifying unmet needs and new ways of meeting them, and in assisting them in building a vocabulary that they can use in their interpersonal relationships that will facilitate discussion rather than argument. While clearly the desired outcome of any therapy should be that the client will reach a point at which he no longer requires it, it should also be clear that if in the future he recognises that he would benefit from more contact with a therapist or facilitator, that there should be no sense of having 'lost a battle' because recognising that one needs help and feeling prepared to ask for that help is representative of greater strength than ignoring the need. Communicating this message requires considerable sensitivity and tact.

The experience of terminating therapy can also be quite different, depending on the form that that therapy has taken. In the case of an open-ended group, in which members join and leave all the time, clients will usually have already had the experience of seeing others leave, and will know what to expect, up to a point. Their peers may experience a range of emotions in association with their leaving, from sensations of relief and encouragement ('If they can do it, so can I') to resistance towards the individual's leaving ('I can't believe Rachel is clearing off now, just as the group is starting to really get going!') especially if they have been a strong member of the group. Part of a therapist's role is to recognise when a client is ready to leave therapy, and to help them to form the decision to do so. Once again, objectivity should be striven for. Even if the client in question is someone who makes a helpful, productive contribution to the group, it is not necessarily in their best interests to remain when the issues that have brought them to therapy have been resolved, even if their presence makes the therapist's task an easier one.

It is not unknown for people leaving therapy to experience some problems as they go through their last few sessions, especially in the case of clients whose underlying issues are related to fear of abandonment. Understandably, many people are afraid that their maladaptive behaviours will re-emerge when they no longer have the support offered by regularly meeting for therapy. The therapist should gently help them in recognising that these implicit protests against the termination of therapy, while perfectly normal, are what they are and no more; that by continuing to practice the appropriate relational needs-getting strategies that they learned in their therapy, they can survive the termination process.

Unplanned termination

We refer to 'unplanned termination' when a client leaves therapy either before the foreseen termination date, or without discussing the prospect of doing so with the therapist and/or group. There are many possible reasons why this may take place from external life factors such as having to move home to other issues such as a lack of comfort within a group or with the therapist herself. Clearly, although no therapist can assume responsibility for her clients, but only for her work, a desired outcome would be to keep unplanned termination to a minimum. Where possible, it would be helpful to meet with the client who terminates prematurely on an individual basis to discuss this decision and to remind the client of the relational needs and emotional triggers that might perpetuate his interpersonal difficulties. In some cases, it may be possible to arrange for the client to attend therapy with another group, individually or with a different therapist.

Possible reactions to planned termination and how to deal with them: Some examples

Certain reactions to termination are commonly felt and expressed, and it is worth describing how these reactions typically present, and how the therapist can help their clients to deal with these difficult emotions.

Sadness

Amy suffered from post natal depression after the birth of her child. She responded well to medical intervention but was left with a feeling of 'emptiness' and was very socially isolated in her role as a stay-at-home mother, having left her job as a dentist's assistant – which she had very much enjoyed – when her child was born. For this reason, she joined a group that offered therapy. Amy's participation in the group was extremely helpful to her. She has been able to identify some practical solutions to her situation – seeking part time work and joining a mothers' group that meets twice a week – and has also learned how better to vocalise her feelings to her 'workaholic' husband. Amy attended a closed group that met for twenty weeks. During the last few weeks, she was notably withdrawn and upset:

'I'm just so sad that the group is ending. It's been a really important social outlet for me. This is the first time I've felt like I've really been myself since Allison was born. Now there's just going to be a great big black hole on Thursday evenings, when I should be here!'

Amy's therapist acknowledges her feelings, and responds by saying:

'Well, I know the group is going to miss you as well, Amy. But it is so great for us all to know that you are much closer to where you want to be, and that you are in a position to make new friends and grow in confidence at your job, in your mothers' group and with Allison. I think I can safely say that seeing you become able to move on has been a big inspiration for us all.'

Here the therapist has validated Amy's competency by enumerating her various, real achievements while making a statement that invites other group members to respond in kind.

Anxiety

Horace, who is nineteen, has been attending an open group because of his problem with substance abuse. Horace's therapist feels that he is ready to stop attending therapy, and Horace agrees, but expresses his fear that things will 'go wrong.'

'I haven't been using for four months, and I have a good job and a girlfriend I really love. But what if I get fired or Natasha dumps me for somebody else? Without the group, who knows if I'll really be able to stay clean?'

Horace's therapist knows that many substance abusers do in fact need to attend several periods of therapy before they are able to get on with life without drugs indefinitely. He is eager to communicate to Horace that attending more therapy is always a possibility for him, without wishing to suggest that Horace is somehow bound to 'fail' the challenges that are now facing him or to imply that, if Horace takes drugs again, that this implies that he is 'a failure' by definition. He says:

'It is 100% normal to be scared by the challenge of facing life without the crutch you've been used to using in the past. But I think that the most important lesson we've learned here is that real support doesn't come from something outside ourselves. It comes from within, and knowing that we will recognise when and if we need to ask for help.'

Here the therapist has acknowledged Horace's fear of abandonment and indirectly suggests that he can prevent these feelings by reaching out himself. Again there is room left for group members to contribute.

Denial

April has been attending an open group providing therapy to people with eating disorders. Although, several weeks ago, she agreed that she was 'almost there' now she arrives at what should be her final therapy session and says: 'I've decided I'm not ready to stop attending. It is way too soon. If I stop now and then go back to the way things were before, I'll be worse off than I was at the outset.'

April's therapist feels that the group has, to some extent, replaced April's addiction to her eating disorder. If he agrees that she should continue with the group rather than leaving, as planned, there is the danger that this will enforce her notion that she can't 'make it on her own' and that her addictive behaviour will become more integral to her own self-image, as food seems to provide April with the reliability that, as has emerged in therapy, she has always experienced as lacking in her personal life. He says:

> 'A lot of people start to wonder if they can make it on their own without outside help. I am sure we all recognise that before coming to this group 'food' was the outside help. But we've all seen what a strong person you are and we are confident that you are going to keep being strong for yourself, even when you have left the group.'

Fear

Robert had been attending a group addressing issues of violence in the home. It is a closed group and, as the therapeutic period draws near a close, Robert becomes increasingly irate.

> 'If I go home and things get out of hand and I end up hitting her,' he yells, 'It'll be your damn fault, not mine. You shouldn't let people think that you can fix them and then turf them out before they are ready!'

Despite Robert's angry tone, it is clear that the potentially more productive emotion here is fear. The therapist does not react strongly to Robert's outburst but, instead, says in a calm tone:

> 'I'm sure the Robert isn't the only one here who is nervous about consistently being able to apply his new skills to his life situation. I guess it is tough to keep in sight the affirmation that we can and will respond to stress without using old ways that didn't work out for us – or anybody else – in the past.'

By identifying Robert's underlying emotion as fear, rather than the anger that he presents with on a more superficial level, and by naming the emotion, the therapist has made it possible to Robert to discuss his feelings without 'backing down' from his expressions of anger, moving forward to a more useful approach to termination.

Relapse

Oliver has been attending a clinic for the morbidly obese and a support group that has been helping its members explore why they eat compulsively, and find ways in which to eat and live in a more healthful manner. Oliver has already lost a lot of weight and his health has improved considerably. He has also made a lot of progress in therapy, identifying the unmet needs that he has been trying to meet by eating. Three weeks ago, Oliver and the therapist agreed that it was almost time for him to 'go out on his own,' but since that date, Oliver has gained twenty pounds and his maladaptive eating habits have apparently returned with a vengeance.

'See?' Oliver says, almost with a note of triumph. *'I haven't really gotten over these 'feeling invisible' issues after all. I've been overeating every day since we met last week. In fact, last night I had two huge Domino's pizzas – with extra cheese, too – and a tub of ice cream. Clearly, I am not yet ready to leave the group.'*

Oliver's relapse is a little worrying, as he initially entered therapy when his family doctor expressed serious concern about his future life expectancy, in view of his extreme weight problem. However, 'allowing' Oliver to choose to return to his previous eating habits would set a dangerous precedent. The therapist says:

'Leaving therapy can be difficult, and a lot of people find that, just before they go out on their own, they react by returning to old ways of meeting their unmet needs. Perhaps we can discuss Oliver's fear of leaving the group and what other options there are for dealing with his fears of not being respected?'

With this, the group begins to explore possibilities for Oliver to be more relationally visible and acknowledged by others. His use of food as a panacea certainly made him more concretely visible to others but, as Oliver seemed to come to understand, his obesity detracted from the respect he so desperately wanted.

Flight

Sarah, an adolescent girl, has been attending group therapy to help her deal with the difficult emotions she has been experiencing around her parents' divorce. Sarah has always engaged well in therapy and has modelled appropriate self-disclosure for some of the more reticent group members. She is a bright, articulate girl. At week ten of the closed, twelve-week group, Sarah calls the therapist and informs her that she will not be finishing therapy, because 'I've got all I can out of it. And it doesn't make any difference anyway.'

Sarah cannot be forced to finish weeks eleven and twelve of the group, but she can be encouraged to do so. If she 'drops out' she may begin to feel that she 'failed' the group and this in turn could have deleterious effects on the difficult emotions she had been experiencing with regard to trust and betrayal. The therapist says:

'That's really too bad, Sarah. You've been a really helpful member of the group and I know that the other members would be sad if you abandoned them so close to 'graduation'. I know you have lots of experience with that feeling and they really benefited from having you around. I hope that you'll reconsider. It is just two more meetings, after all.'

Tools to take to the world

The goal and purpose of the Needs ABC model is, of course, to help clients achieve emotional wellness, and not to provide the therapist with an 'easy way out.' The desired outcome of therapy is always for that therapy to become obsolete, even if this is not always possible after just one series of meetings. It is important to encourage clients to work towards a time when they will be able to work to meet their needs on their own in a productive manner; in other words, to become enabled to 'be their own therapist' and find solutions on their own.

That said, it is also true that many clients will need to attend therapy again, and it should also be clear that, if this is the case, they should not feel that they are 'failures' but to understand that they are simply involved in a process of tailoring their needs acquisition strategies to their own styles of problem-solving. Indeed; old, tried and true behaviours are hard to give up, especially at times of emotional crisis. Most of us would rather feel in control of our environment than give others that control at most any time. Rotter[43] has suggested that, within social learning theory, a generalised expectancy related to internal versus external control of reinforcement – locus of control – is that of 'looking for alternatives.' Rotter suggests that psychotherapy clients may be taught to look for alternatives to their problematic behaviours. If a client feels that they have hit an obstacle that they cannot overcome, they are at risk of relapse into the behaviours that have proven 'effective' in the past, even though they have also been associated with many problems – the very problems that brought them to therapy in the first place. Sometimes, all these clients need is a reminder of how to gain some objectivity with respect to what is going on in their lives. There will be times when a return to a Needs ABC treatment for a 'tune-up' provides a good strategy. Certainly, the more engrained the old behaviours are, the more difficult it will be to extinguish them and the more time effective problem-solving is likely to take. In some cases, clients can acquire the time they need to work on the underlying emotions and the related behaviours that are proving problematic by attending a different form of treatment with the aim of fine-tuning the strategies that they have learned in therapy. For instance, on terminating group therapy, some clients will find a period of individual therapy useful. Throughout therapy, the therapist should consistently model patience and understand each client's reality in order to be able to help them progress with their lives in a productive, healthy way.

11
Student supervision

THE NEEDS ABC model has much to offer the student in preparation for becoming a therapist in terms of helping them to develop their knowledge and skills and the empathy and objectivity required to assist clients in moving forward with their lives minus the maladaptive behaviours that have brought them to therapy. By incorporating the best of previously established therapeutic approaches in a package that can readily be adapted to individual therapist style and specific client needs, the Needs ABC model provides an excellent template for the therapist in the making.

Teachers and students

The dynamic between students and their supervisors is key to how the former develop as caring professionals. Especially important during the learning process is that students are given the opportunity to put their new knowledge into practice in a real situation; in the context of providing therapy. In the therapeutic environment, supervisors also have the opportunity to model appropriate interventions and disclosures.

In the context of training, students must be helped to explore issues relating to gender, power, control, stereotypes and socialisation while receiving the support they need throughout what can be a challenging time. Student progress, like client progress, occurs as goals are attained and understanding grows.

Of course, nothing prepares a student as well for a professional standing as a counsellor as actual interaction with therapy clients. Some students become qualified to interact with clients on a professional level by virtue of their academic achievement, but in order to prepare them for a future practice of their own, it is essential that they receive hands-on training from people who are already experienced in this field.

Practical issues that surround the question of student training include whether or not the students will provide therapeutic leadership with their supervisor in the room or not, and if not, how and when the supervisors will have access to the therapeutic unit 'in action' so as to be able to provide valuable feedback to the student. One option is for supervisors to observe the group from behind a one-way mirror, while others include live supervision and the use of video taping. This can be experienced as intrusive by some clients (who must, of course, be informed that they are being observed) but with honesty and the provision of explanations as to why this approach is important, most clients are able to accept this scenario.

The supervision of students can be carried out in a group and/or in an individual format, with regular meetings between supervisor and student. Students need to be assisted in exploring not just issues pertaining to their clients, but also, when necessary, their personal issues relating to their own development and background. These issues will inevitably be brought to bear on how they interact with the people who come to them for therapy. Where communication difficulties arise as a result of a therapist's inability to be completely objective – because of something in their own background – these difficulties will need to be identified, recognised, and compensated for appropriately. When students are preparing to become group therapists, in particular, group supervision can be especially apt, as it provides a scenario whereby appropriate, productive group behaviour can be modelled to the students.

Being a student the Needs ABC way

Typically, students will get to know the Needs ABC model after they have acquired a considerable amount of theoretical material in the context of training to be a social worker, psychologist or other helping professional. They will already be familiar with the background to therapy and with many of the primary psychotherapeutic models. What they now need to do is understand how to apply their theoretical knowledge to a real therapeutic situation. The best way to enable them to do this is to engage in a supervisory process, which will frame the therapeutic strategies used in this setting by modelling important and appropriate problem-solving interventions. The supervisory process can be seen as collaborative, cooperative, and inclusive – much like the model itself. In preparing to become group therapists, students are also trained in a group environment that models the therapeutic environment quite closely.

The developmental stages of the supervision group mirror the stages of treatment, and the safety of the intern – both emotional and practical – is important in order to support the learning process. Students will have to acknowledge their vulnerabilities and learn to use different problem solving strategies. Student growth must be monitored and maintained on an individual basis while encouraging and perpetuating positive movement in the supervision group. Therefore, in as much as students tend to be concerned about their competency in an internship, it would be important for a Needs ABC student to understand whether this is an important need for the student to acquire, or an artefact of their anxiety about doing well as a student. As well, it would be important for the student to examine their important relational needs so as not to confuse what they need in their own relationships with what the client is asking. Finally, Needs ABC interns would be encouraged to examine the possibilities of how their relational needs might interfere with their work, and develop strategies accordingly.

Initially, students in preparation to become therapists can often feel vulnerable, just as new members of group therapy do. However, they should be made aware that this vulnerability can become a strength, in creating a better awareness of the vulnerability of their clients. The training process will, in fact, provide them with many points of connection with future members of their therapeutic units. As they implement ways to help their clients feel more at ease in the therapeutic environment, they will be able to recall their own anxieties during the early stages of training.

Training as a group

Students who are planning to becoming group therapists unsurprisingly benefit greatly from training in a group context. By inviting students to co-supervise and modelling as co-supervisors in a group supervision context, the students are taught a model of cooperative co-therapy. Group process can also be used to help the student move forward in the same way as the clients, giving them great insight into what being a member of a therapeutic group is truly like. As in all treatment milieus, students must deal with their own concerns and misgivings about issues including competence, competition, gender issues, family of origin issues and the difficulties of collaboration.

Collaboration resides in the unique interactive quality of the team, which achieves a balance between control and support and depends on the ability to develop trust. Supervisors must model appropriate strategies to promote group cohesion and balance. They must be open about their own fears and vulnerabilities, thus allowing for the acceptance of 'not knowing' as an essential quality for continuous learning, improvement and effectiveness. Co-supervision includes sharing, which relieves isolation and makes visible what otherwise might remain invisible. It is crucial to encourage a spirit of mutual learning and, since we each learn about ourselves in working with another supervisor, this relationship becomes a partnership that requires honest and open dialogue and the safety and comfort to disagree with one another. From a social work perspective, decision-making takes for granted the need for collaboration and dialogue. Thus, the supervisor-supervisor as well as the supervisor-supervisee relationship models the therapist-client one.

Examining a case study will provide some insight into student supervision of future Needs ABC therapists:

Example: George

George was the only male member of a group therapy team that a Needs ABC therapist was supervising. He was the co-facilitator of a mixed group of men and women who had separated from their partners because of infidelity. His co-therapy partner was Mary, while the other two women, Sheila and Rosemary, co-facilitated a woman's group for single mothers. All therapy sessions were video-taped and portions of them were reviewed once a week when the therapy teams felt there were problems or concerns about specific clients or situations within the groups. Over the course of several weeks, I noticed that George seemed to be taking a prominent position in his group, apparently invalidating and marginalising Mary's role in the treatment. At this point, after viewing a portion of George and Mary's group where there was concern about a male client's behaviour, I asked the team about how they seemed to view the dynamics of the co-facilitation between George and Mary. Rosemary stated that she felt they were a good team but that George was 'a little too strong' in the group. Sheila, after a moment of consideration, said, *'You know, George, I really like the way you support our team but I have been a little concerned, lately, that you are modelling a bit too much patriarchy.'*

At that, George enquired: *'What do you mean? You know I try to work from a feminist perspective.'*

Rosemary added, *'I see what Sheila is talking about. I'm sure you're not doing it on purpose but it is almost as if you need to have the upper hand.'* Mary finally spoke up, saying, *'Yep, I have to admit it, at times I felt almost shut out of the discussion but* (looking at George) *you did such a good job that I thought, "what the heck."'*

At this point, the leader jumped in, suggesting, *'Why don't we replay that portion of the tape and you can point out exactly where you see this happening and make suggestions for more appropriate options. What do you think, George?'*

George nodded in agreement and the group proceeded to view the tape. Though Sheila and Rosemary took a more active role, Mary joined in with suggestions on how she would have felt more supported and acknowledged in her facilitation role. George, a little shyly, offered the following once the review was completed, *'I'm sorry, Mary, but I guess 'competency' is a big button for me. It is really important for me to do well this year* and I guess I am trying to show everyone how much I have learned.' Then, with a nervous smile, he added, *'I don't want my successes to be overlooked, but I certainly did not want to be noticed at your expense.'* Mary said, *'Believe me, George, I didn't take this personally. I suppose I should have been more assertive, but I guess "competency" is also one of the issues I have to work on as well.'* At this point, the leader remembered from our initial meetings, when Mary and George had applied to the team, that George had felt marginalised and inadequate in his marriage (he was a divorcé) and Mary stated that one of her goals was to be more assertive and feel better about her abilities as a therapist. If the team had not handled this so well, the leader would have met with George and Mary individually to discuss and work through their needs as helping professionals.

Limit setting is one of the important dilemmas that must be dealt within supervision. It is often difficult for students who feel as if they are failures if their clients do not succeed in reaching their goals. It is through supervision that students can slowly begin to understand what their responsibility is and what responsibility belongs to the client. By understanding how relational needs impinge upon decision-making, supervisors can help their students set appropriate limits by helping them to understand what is possible or acceptable and what is not, thereby identifying what is most helpful to the client. This will empower the student, and in turn the client, to take appropriate action rather than creating dependency.

12
Final comments

HUMAN BEINGS ARE not automata. This, of course, includes therapists. There is no one-size-fits-all approach to therapy, and each therapist will have to evolve and continue to evolve their own approach and framework to therapy. That said, the Needs ABC approach to therapy provides a very helpful, gender- and ethnicity-neutral basis on which to build one's own approach, precisely because it is flexible, non-directive, non-judgemental, and has the potential to adapt to a wide range of situations, client types, personalities, and therapeutic environments. Even though factors that impinge upon the client might differ radically from one individual to another, and predict different relational needs and competencies, the therapeutic strategies of this model will remain the same. Particularly in the case of the Needs ABC therapy being applied in a group setting, this approach creates a microcosm of society, in which positive behaviours can be modelled and emotions explored. This is as true in the case of involuntary clients as it is in the case of those who present themselves for therapy autonomously.

By focussing on the emotionally laden relational needs behind the dysfunctional behaviours that have brought clients to therapy rather than on the behaviours themselves, therapists enable their clients to remove themselves from the cycle of self-blame/guilt/unhappiness/dysfunctional behaviours that is so very hard to break out of. The core assumption of the model is that 'bad' or maladaptive behaviour is displayed by people because they are attempting, however unsuccessfully, to fulfil unmet emotional needs. We can state this best by saying that the best way to work on a problem is not to work on the problem. The best way is to work on the reason for the problem. Clients need to be made aware of what I have to come refer to as the Needs ABC Law of Relationships: Whenever you use a dysfunctional behaviour to solve a problem you always get exactly what you do not want!

In utilising the Needs ABC approach, therapists assist their clients to become integral to the process of therapy so that they experience themselves as in charge of their own situation, fostering a sensation of power and self-authority and enabling them to take responsibility for their own behaviours and explore the emotions behind them.

The purpose of therapy the Needs ABC way is to discover the unmet needs experienced by the client, and understand how and why these lead to the behaviours that are causing the problem or problems in his life. Once a client has come to recognise and accept the unmet needs that lie behind his maladaptive behaviours, a huge leap has been taken towards the attainment of emotional wellness. But the task of the therapist and the client is not over yet. Change itself is an anxiety-causing situation, and the therapist will need to provide her clients with the practical and emotional support they need as they do what they need to do to create changes in their personal and family relationships.

In order to create an arena of trust, the group work, family, couple, or individual therapeutic environment should provide a supportive framework ensuring the emotional safety of the individual or individuals seeking help. The Needs ABC model focuses on the creation of a safe, predictable environment that makes sharing feelings easier for the participant and also reflects the sort of environment that they need and want to carve out for themselves in the wider world.

Sometimes, the challenge of creating change in one's life is too big to be achieved after one course of therapy. While the goal of the Needs ABC approach to therapy is its own redundancy, as clients achieve their therapy goals, those clients who do need to return to therapy should not feel that they are failures in any way, but experience themselves as recognised for having the courage to continue their quest. Overall, a key asset of the Needs ABC approach is the provision to clients of a safe environment to which they can return in the case of future need. The challenge of this model for the therapist to draw from his own life experiences in order to be able to have the empathy required to identify both the emotional need as well as the emotion that arises from not getting it met. The primary difficulty for therapists, therefore, would be around not wanting to look at their own emotional experiences, as this might conjure up difficult emotions for them as well. Allowing himself to connect with the client around emotional issues without becoming intrusive might present a challenge for the therapist who is unaccustomed to working with the emotional component of the treatment. Examples of this would include psychoanalysts who tend to make interpretations as pronunciations at the end of each session rather than engaging with the client, object relations theorists who are trained to describe individuals as 'objects' rather than persons, or cognitive-behaviouralists who tend to look at relationships in terms of behavioural patterns that can be measured and then modified by changing they way in which one thinks about a situation concretely.

The Needs ABC approach is not just an approach to conducting therapy in the context of formally arranged settings; it calls for a shift in outlook and insight that has implications for every aspect of the therapeutic experience, from the first moment of contact between therapist and client – which is properly considered the onset of therapy – to the termination of therapy. At all times, the focus is on emotional safety for the client, and the uncovering on the emotions that lie behind counterproductive behaviours. Therapists must maintain an exquisite awareness of the nuances in client narrative in order to posit explanations vis a vis underlying emotion and make these emotions more accessible to the client. They should be ready and able to support clients who will inevitably have to experience a certain amount of discomfort in recognising difficult emotions and taking responsibility for unproductive behaviours, while assuring them in word and in action that they are in a safe environment where disclosure will not be punished and providing them with a goal to work towards from an early point in the therapy, so that there is a clear purpose to the client's engagement with their therapist and, in the case of therapy, with the group. In this manner, the client is helped to 'take charge' of their own life, and the things that they feel are missing from it. In this context, it is helpful for the Needs ABC therapist to realise that, frequently, clients' apparent resistance to change and to the therapy that may lead to change, is related to anxiety about the task facing them and/or resentment about being in therapy at all. Anxiety and resistance can be minimised if it is clear from the outset that the therapeutic environment – regardless of the composition of the therapeutic unit – is safe, if the therapy goals and methods are transparent and understandable, and if the therapists are demonstrably able to perform their role.

The Needs ABC approach is flexible and facilitates the utilisation of a wide range of tools to assist clients in opening up, including the judicious use of modelling and self-disclosure, both on the part of the therapist and, in group and family therapy, on the part of clients. When appropriate, it can accommodate a certain amount of 'wandering' from the theme at hand; the Needs ABC therapist knows that there are times when it can be useful to deflect tension or to allow clients to express themselves on topics not immediately obviously related to the core issues presenting for therapy. The therapist will need to learn how to tread the fine line between intervening just enough and not too much, especially in the case of therapeutic units involving various clients, such as group or family therapy.

Needs ABC: Acquisition and Behaviour Change

The Needs ABC approach rests on the understanding that regardless of differences in age, ethnicity, gender and social standing the fundamentals of human experience are remarkably similar from one individual to the next. People may use different vocabularies and express themselves with different behaviours but, on examination, these tend to be demonstrably related to a relatively small number of underlying 'issues.' This in turn means that an individual client's underlying issues – referred to throughout this book as 'universal themes' – can be presented to the other individuals attending therapy and discussed using a vocabulary that all clients will be able to relate to. Thus, rather than discussing clients' specific problems, members of a therapeutic unit work with concepts of fear of abandonment, isolation and so forth. Universalising issues in this manner makes it possible for solutions to be sought and found without using a too-narrow focus on the specifics on any given client's situation, deflecting blame and recrimination and making it easier to work towards a meaningful approach. It also reduces the risk of damaging clients' often fragile self-esteem by maintaining a general focus and leads the client towards a process that will result in his acquiring a better understanding of his emotional issues, and how he can deal with them better. In fact, even though a client's need might at first seem specific to a particular situation, it can be generalised to the way the client reacts to the rest of the world. The therapist can generally recognise real steps forward when clients start becoming able to discuss their underlying emotions using different words and a fresh understanding, indicating that movement has taken place. It should be noted that all of the above applies equally in closed and open group therapy, family and couples therapy and in individual therapy. As therapy progresses, careful use of interventions including supportive challenging, modelling and mentoring – by one client for another, or by the therapist for the client – can assist. As well, therapists can use linking techniques to assist clients in seeing how their needs are similar, or engage in group linking by highlighting issues that seem to be common to the whole therapeutic unit. All the while, the therapist should bear in mind that work should be carried out at the clients' own pace, that progress will not always be uniform, and that it is essential that the therapeutic unit should not try to work to some sort of a timetable or stricture. In utilising universal themes – both those provided here and those that emerge in the context of each therapist's own experience – all of the above can be made easier in providing a vocabulary and a clear frame of reference within which to work.

Universal themes – the themes that describe the needs that underlie behaviour – generally relate to issues that originally emerged in childhood, especially during the latency period, when the individual's personality was largely formed. Consequently, it is useful to explore their experiential background with clients so as to understand, preferably without laying blame at anybody's door, where their personal emotional needs originated.

As universal themes are explored, it is important to be aware that, while the themes are universal, different people will express them in different ways, depending in part on issues of culture and gender. The therapist will need to endeavour to become familiar with at least a general understanding of the cultures of his clients, and the various ways in which they may say essentially the same thing. At the same time, one should not overlook the fact that similar behaviours – alcoholism, interspousal violence, eating disorders, or whatever – can spring from different themes. The therapist should remember that stated emotions are often underlain by other, more useful emotions – fear or sadness can mask anger, for example – that can motivate clients to action. With this understanding, the therapist can validate clients' feelings without condoning behaviours that are inappropriate or damaging and can move from exploring and understanding these feelings and their origin to devising new and more useful behavioural reactions to them. In the process, there are some key factors that should always be avoided, namely focusing on one client in a group to the exclusion of others, by focusing on the overt element of client narrative rather than the underlying themes or by using sarcasm or confrontation and in using it to provide clients with feedback and observations about their behaviour. As well, in the context of a therapeutic unit containing several individuals, it is crucial to bear in mind that clients will not all progress at a uniform rate.

Let us return back to the beginning of the book and revisit the case of Ethel. You might remember that Ethel was the woman who was asked to leave by her husband for continuing to drink despite his pleas to remember her allegiance to the family. In fact, Ethel and Ted did finally reconcile and, during the couple therapy that they engaged in following Ted's decision to 'reconsider and take her back,' loyalty turned out to be an important relational need for him. Here's how it happened:

> During Ethel's treatment, she discovered that her feelings of being disrespected or marginalised arose from a felt sense of incompetency. Ethel felt that she was ineffective at problem-solving in her relationships. Her self-doubts seemed to promote a lack of appropriate assertiveness, leading her to object passive-aggressively through the use of alcohol. As her treatment progressed, Ethel's group work peers helped her to focus on her relational needs. These seemed to most powerfully involve Ethel's relationship with herself. In one group session, the following interaction occurred:
>
> *Ethel had, once again, bemoaned her fate with regard to losing her family*

Needs ABC: Acquisition and Behaviour Change

and having no place to go. Another group member, Cathy, jumped in saying, 'It's not your drinking that's the problem. You just don't think there's any other way to handle your situation. And you know what? You are right. You can't do a thing about what your husband has done. Why don't you look at what you can do to help you in the rest of your life? I'm tired of the broken record.'

Pauline, another group member, jumped in and said: 'Cathy, don't be so hard on her. She's lost a lot. I do hope she will be able to move past her husband's power over her and get her own power, but she needs time. Maybe she can do some individual work after she leaves here. It seems that Ethel's husband wants her to get as much help as she can.'

Angrily, Ethel declared: *'I have had enough! I can't do any more therapy. Every time I get into a relationship I feel inadequate. Screw them, and screw you, Pauline. You're always Miss Nicey-nice. Do this! Do that! You're a doormat's doormat! I am going to swear off men ... forever! I'll just live alone for the rest of my life.'*

With that the therapist jumped in saying: *'I think Ethel might have turned a corner, thanks to Pauline.'* With this other group members validated Ethel's anger as a motivating factor in the development of Ethel's autonomy and potential for individuation from the men in her life. As time went on it seemed evident that competency – Ethel's fear of being incompetent – was a major factor in her ability to get the recognition she felt she deserved. In one group she stated: *'Maybe if I was better at what I needed to do people would pay more attention to me.'*

As time went on Ethel was able to complete her treatment with the goal of 'making a go of it alone.' Her ability to demonstrate her independence seemed to interest Ted. He seemed to become hopeful when she informed him that she respected his decision and didn't continue to 'pester' him as she did in the past. She got a job and developed her own social support system and when Ted, after about a six month hiatus, 'bumped into her' with some female friends at a movie, he asked her to have coffee with him to 'talk things over.' It was at this accidental meeting that Ted suggested they try again with couple counselling as a proviso for determining if they should reunite. It seems that Ted had not had any meaningful relationships since Ethel left, having devoted most of his free time to parenting the children. In addition, it seems that his kids really missed Ethel – the Ethel they knew when she wasn't drinking.

Even though Ethel went to counselling with Ted only reluctantly at first, it soon became clear that she would not continue to be punished for 'the ghosts of Christmas past' but rather supported for maintaining and improving her autonomy. The therapist did ally with Ted around his dedication to his children and to his need to support his family financially in the best way he could. The therapist also supported Ethel's need for emotional reliability. Some suggestions about how they could rebuild their relational trust and improve their connection to one-another included Ethel's spending time with the children and taking care of them (with his ex's permission) when Ted was away for long periods of time. This would help Ethel with her need to feel competent and respected while improving her connection with Ted's children (who did miss her after all). Ted offered to call her more often while on the road as long as she was clear that it wasn't to check up on her, but to validate his love for her.

After about four months of therapy the couple terminated their treatment. In an e-mail that Ethel sent to their couple therapist on the 'anniversary' of her leaving her inpatient treatment she indicated that all was going well. She stated that she still became angry and frightened at times about her relationship with Ted but managed to continue to work up the courage to speak to Ted about how she felt, as well as acknowledging what relational need was being challenged when she felt that way. She had stated that Ted continued to support her assertiveness and that she was beginning to believe that she is a worthy partner and stepmother. In an impressive display of maturity, Ethel has been able to have a good working relationship with Ted's children's mother.

Knowing as a therapist that one has been instrumental in a client's becoming able to take control of their own life is deeply rewarding, but the Needs ABC approach is not about the therapist's need for feeling empowered in her role. It is about making it possible for people to become stronger, happier versions of themselves.

Notes

1. Doel, M. (2006) pp.4-5.
2. Caliso, J.A. and Milner, J.S. (1994),; Egeland, B. (1993) n R.J. Gelles and D.R. Loseke (eds); Fry, D.P. (1993).
3. To avoid using the rather awkward 's/he' or 'he or she' constructs, we will use 'he' and 'she' randomly when referring to group work clients.
4. Adam Blatner (2005) notes that precursors to group therapy can be traced to as early as the seventeenth century, while 'scientific' approaches began to emerge in the early years of the twentieth century.
5. Dennis, M. et al (2004).
6. Kurland, R. and Salmon, R. (1992).
7. Ellis, A. (1997)
8. See for example Miller, W. & Rollnick, S. (1991).
9. Anderson, H. (1993); Carr, Alan (1998).
10. Miller, S. and Greenburg, L. (1988).
11. Doel, M. (2006). p. 31
12. Patterson, J. et al. (1998)
13. Patterson, J. et al (1998); Johnson, S. (2004).
14. Mohl, P.C., Martinez, D., Ticknor, C., Huang, M., Cordell L. (1991); Noel, S.B., Howard, K.I. K.I. (1989).
15. Wickham, E. 1993, p. 69.
16. Yalom, I. (1995).
17. Yalom, I. (1995) p. 119.
18. Yalom, I. (1995) p. 130.
19. Garland, J., Jones, H. and Kolodny, R. (1978)
20. Smith, M.K. (1995)
21. Currie, D. (1983)
22. Buckley, L.B. Miller, D. and Rolfe, T.A. (1983)
23. Schiller, L. (1995)
24. Previously published discussions of the N·ABC, developed by Tom Caplan, were co-authored with Harle Thomas, who provided input into the areas involving client states and universal themes. Thomas, my initial collaborator, helped me to put many of the original concepts of this model into writing. He helped to express

many of the ideas that needed conceptualizing including the initial version of the 'Universal Themes,' the labeling of the group stages, and the concepts of 'supportive challenging' and differentiating between 'comfort' and 'safety'.

25. Yalom, I. (2005) p. 416
26. Yalom, I. (2005)
27. Almeida R.V. and Bograd, M. (1990)
28. Freud, S. (1905)
29. Freud, A.(1930)
30. Erikson, E. (1956)
31. This subsection owes a great deal to the previously published paper, Caplan, T. & Thomas, H. (2004). If we are all in the same canoe, why are we using different paddles? The effective use of common themes in diverse group situations. *Social Work with Groups.* 27(1), 53-73.
32. Caplan, T. & Thomas, H. (2004).
33. Adapted from AADAC Parent Information Series www.aadac.com
34. he following is derived from the following article by Caplan and Thomas (2004): If We Are All in the Same Canoe, Why Are We Using Different Paddles: The Effective Use of Common Themes in Diverse Group Situations, *Social Work With Groups*, 27(1)
35. Greenberg L. and Johnson, S. (1988). Adapted from their terminology, which refers to 'primary' and 'secondary' emotion.
36. Greenberg L. and Johnson, S. (1988).
37. Kurland, R. and Salmon, R. (1992)
38. Mosak, H.H. (1987)
39. Tolstoy, L. (2003, orig. 1877)
40. Greenberg L. and Johnson, S. (1988), p.18.
41. Yalom, I. (2005). p. 361.
42. Rotter, J.B. (1978).

Bibliography/references

Almeida, R.V., and Bograd, M. (1990) Sponsorship: Holding men accountable for domestic violence, Journal of feminist family therapy, 2(3/4), pp. 243-259.

Anderson, C. and Stewart, S. (1983) Mastering resistance: A practical guide to family therapy. New York: Guilford Press.

Anderson, H. (1993) On a roller coaster: A collaborative language systems approach to therapy. In S. Friedman (Eds.), The language of change. New York: Guilford.

Ansbacher, H.L. and R.R. (1967) The individual psychology of Alfred Adler. Heinz L. New York: Harper and Row.

Bandura, A. (1997) Self-efficacy: The exercise of control. New York: W.H. Freeman.

Blatner, A. (2005) A historical chronology of group psychotherapy and psychodrama. Retrieved online from http://www.blatner.com/adam/pdntbk/hxgrprx.htm. Substantially derived from Blatner's Appendix A in his 1988 Foundations of Psychodrama.

Brown, T.G., Werk, A., Caplan, T., & Seraganian, P. (2003) Violent substance abusers in domestic violence treatment. In R. Csiernik and W. Rowe (Eds.), Responding to the oppression of addiction. Toronto: Canadian Scholars' Press Inc.

Buckley, L.B., Miller, D. and Rolfe, T.A. (Fall-Winter, 1983) A Windsor model. Social work with groups, 6(3/4), 189-195.

Caliso, J.A. and Milner, J.S. (1994) Childhood physical abuse, childhood social support, and adult child abuse potential, Journal of interpersonal violence, vol.9, no.1, 27-44.

Caplan, T. and Thomas, H. (2004) If we are all in the same canoe, why are we using different paddles? The effective use of common themes in diverse group situations. Social work with groups. 27(1), 53-73.

Caplan, T. and Thomas, H. (2004) If this is week three, we must be doing 'feelings:' An essay on the importance of client-paced group work. Social work with groups 26(3), 5-15.

Caplan, T. and Thomas, H. (2002) The forgotten moment: Therapeutic resilience and its promotion in social work with groups. Social work with groups, 24(2), 5-26.

Caplan, T., and Thomas, H. (1997-1998) 'Don't worry, it's just a stage he's going through:' A reappraisal of the stage theory of group work as applied to an open treatment group for men who abuse women. Group work, 10(3), 231-250.

Caplan, T., and Thomas, H. (1995) Safety and comfort, content and process: Facilitating open group work for men who batter. Social work with groups, 18 (2/3), 33-51.

Caplan, T, and Werk, A. (1994) Therapeutic dilemmas in group work with men who abuse their partners. Intervention, 98 (6), 54-61.

Caplan, T. (2005) Active or passive interventions in groups: The group leader's dilemma. GroupWork. Vol. 15(1), 25-42.

Carr, Alan (1998). Michael White's narrative therapy. Contemporary family therapy, 20 (4), 485-501.

Currie, D., (1983) The Toronto model. Social work with groups 6: 179–188.

de Shazer, S. (1985) Keys to solution in brief therapy. New York: Norton.

Dennis et al., (2005) The duration and correlates of additional and treatment careers. Journal of substance abuse treatment, 28.

Doel, M. and Sawdon, S. (1999) The essential groupworker: Teaching and learning creative group work. London: Jessica Kingsley Publishers Ltd.

Doel, M., (2006) Using Groupwork. London: Routledge.

Egeland, B. (1993) A history of abuse is a major risk factor for abusing the next generation, in Gelles R.J. and Loseke D.R. (eds) Current controversies on family violence. California: Sage Publications.

Ellis, A., & MacLaren, C. (1992) Rational emotive behaviour therapy: A group facilitator's guide. Toronto: Allyn and Bacon.

Ellis, A. (1997) The practice of rational emotive behaviour therapy. New York: Springer Publishing Company.

Emmons, K. M. & Rollnick, S. (2001) Motivational interviewing in health care settings: opportunities and limitations. American journal of preventive medicine, 20(1), 68-74.

Erikson, E.H. (1950) Childhood and Society. New York: Norton.

Erikson, E.H. (1956) The problem of ego identity., J. Amer. Psychoanal. Assn., 4:56-121.

Erikson, E.H. (1956) Ego identity and the psychosocial moratorium. In H.L. Witmer and R. Rosinsky (Eds.) New perspectives for research in juvenile delinquency. U.S. Children's Bureau: Publication 356, pp. 1-23.

Freud, A. (1930) The latency period. Writings, 1:105-120.

Freud, Sigmund (1996) Drei Abhandlungen zur Sexualtheorie. Fischer: Frankfurt am Main. Reprint of the 1905 edition.

Freud, S. (1913) The Interpretation of Dreams (Brill, A.A., Trans.). New York: Macmillan. (Original work published 1900)

Froberg, W. and Slife, B.D. (July, 1987) Overcoming obstacles to the implementation of Yalom's model of inpatient group psychotherapy. International journal of group psychotherapy, 37 (3), 371-388.

Fry, D.P. (1993) The intergenerational transmission of disciplinary practices to conflict human organisation, vol.52, no.2, 176-185.

Garland, J., Jones, H., and Kolodny, R. (1978) A model for stages of development in social work groups, in Bernstein, S. (ed.) Explorations in Group Work: Essays in Theory and Practice, Boston, Boston University School of Social Work

Garvin, C. (1974) Group process: Usage and uses in social work practice. In Glasser, P., Sarri, R., Vinter R.,(Eds.) Individual change through small groups. New York: Free Press.

Gladding, S. T. (1999) Group work: A counseling specialty. (3rd ed) Upper Saddle River, New Jersey: Prentice Hall.

Goldberg Wood, G. & Middleman, R. (1992) Recasting the dye: A small group approach to giving batterers a chance to change. Social work with groups, 15 (1), 5-18.

Goldstein, W. (1999) Practical questions beginning psychotherapy. Psychiatric times. Vol. X, VI, Issue 4. Retrieved from http://www.psychiatrictimes.com/p990447.html

Greenberg, L.S. and Pavio, S.C. (1997) Working with emotions in psychotherapy. New York: Guilford Press.

Greenberg, L. and Johnson, S. (1988) Emotionally focused couples therapy. New York: Guilford Press.

Haley, J. (1991) Problem-solving therapy. San Francisco: Jossey-Bass.

Greenson, R.R. (1967) The technique and practice of psychoanalysis. New York: International Universities Press.

Jacobson, S. (1984) A component analysis of behavioural marital therapy: The relative effectiveness of behaviour exchange and problem solving training. Journal of consulting and clinical psychology, 52, 295–305.

Jenkins, A. (1990) Invitations to responsibility. Adelaide, South Australia: Dulwich Centre Publications.

Johnson, S. (2004) The practice of emotionally focused couples therapy. New York: Brunner-Routledge.

Kurland, R. and Salmon, R. (1992) Group work vs. case work in a group: Principles and applications for teaching in practice. Social work for groups. Vol. 15 (4). 3-14.

Avis, J. M. (2004) Narrative Ideas in Clinical Practice. Workshop given at the University of Guelph on November 5.

Liebenberg, B. (March, 1983) The group therapist and the patient: Countertransference and resistance in group psychotherapy. Smith College studies in social work, 53 (2), 85-102.

Maione, P.V and Chenail, R.J. (2004) Qualitative inquiry in psychotherapy: Research on the common factors. In Hubble, M.A., Duncan, B.L., and Miller, S.D., (Eds.), The heart and soul of change: What works in therapy. Washington, DC: American Psychological Association

Malekoff, A. (1997) Group work with adolescents: Principles and practice. New York:

Guilford.

Miller, W & Rollnick, S. (1991) Motivational interviewing: Preparing people to change addictive behaviour. New York: The Guildford Press.

Mohl, P.C., Martinez, D., Ticknor, C., Huang, M., Cordell L. (1991) Early dropouts from psychotherapy. Journal of nervous mental disorders. Aug. 179(8):478-81.

Mosak, H. H. (1987) Ha ha and aha: The role of humor in psychotherapy. London: Taylor and Francis.

Mullender, A. and Ward, D. (1991) Self-Directed Group work: action for empowerment. London: Whiting & Birch.

Nichols, M., & Schwartz, R. (1991) Family therapy: Concepts and methods. Toronto: Allyn and Bacon.

Noel, S.B., Howard, K.I. K.I. (1989) Initial contact and engagement in psychotherapy. Journal of clinical psychology. Sept. 45(5):798-805.

Nuttall, C. (2005) Counselling London: The first step. Retrieved from http://www.carynnuttall.co.uk/.

Orlinsky, D., Grawe, K. and Parks, B. (1994) Process and outcome in psychotherapy: Noch einmal. in A. Bergin and S. Garfield (Eds). The handbook of psychotherapy and behaviour change. (4th Ed) Toronto: Wiley.

Ormont, R.L. (1993). Resolving resistances to immediacy in the group setting. International Journal of Group Psychotherapy, 43 (4), 399-418.

Patterson, J., Williams, L., Grauf-Grounds, C., and Chamow, L. (1998). Essential skills in family therapy: From the first interview to termination. New York: Guilford Publications

Pretzer, J.L., & Walsh, C.A. (2001). Optimism, pessimism, and psychotherapy: Implications for clinical practice. In Chang E.C. (Ed.), Optimism and pessimism: Implications for theory, research, and practice (pp. 321-346). Washington, DC: American Psychological Association.

Rose, S. D. (1989) Working with adults in groups. San Francisco: Jossey-Bass.

Rotter, J. B. (1978) Generalized expectancies for problem solving and psychotherapy. Cognitive therapy and research, 2, 1-10.

Schiller, L. (1995) Stages of development in women's groups: A relational model. In R. Kurland and R. Salmon, (Eds.) Group work practice in a troubled society: Problems and opportunities. New York: Haworth Press. 117-138

Shulman, L. (1992) The skills of helping: Individuals, families and groups. Itasca Ill.: F.E. Peacock Publishers.

Smith, M. K. (2005) Bruce W. Tuckman – forming, storming, norming and performing in groups, the encyclopaedia of informal education. Retrieved from www.infed.org/thinkers/tuckman.htm.

Thomas, H. & Caplan, T. (1997). Client, therapist and context: Addressing resistance in group work. The social worker, 65 (3), 27-36.

Thomas, H., & Caplan, T. (1999) Spinning the group process wheel: Effective facilitation techniques for motivating involuntary client groups. Social Work with Groups, 21(4), 3-21.

Tolstoy, L. (2003, orig. 1877) Anna Karenina. Penguin Classics.

Toseland, R.W. & Rivas, R.F. (2005) An introduction to group work practice (5th Ed.). Toronto: Pearson Education Inc.

Verhulst, J.C.R.M. & van de Vijver, F.J.R. (April, 1990) Resistance during psychotherapy and behaviour therapy. Behaviour modification, 14 (2), 172-187.

Vinogradov, S. & Yalom, I.D. (1989) A concise guide to group psychotherapy. Washington, DC: American Psychiatric Press.

Werk, A., & Caplan, T. (1998) Non-violent group supervision within a violence clinic context. The clinical supervisor, 17 (2), 101-111.

Westra, H.A., Boardman, C, Moran-Tynski, S. (2000) The impact of providing pre-assessment information on no-show rates. Journal of psychiatry. Aug. 45 (6):572.

White, M., & Epston, D. (1990) Narrative means to therapeutic ends. New York: Norton.

Wickham, E. (1993) Group treatment in social work: An integration of theory and practice. Thompson Educational Publishing.

Yalom, I.D. (1998) Inside therapy: Illuminating writings about group facilitators, patients, and psychotherapy (I. Rabinowitz, Ed.). New York: St. Martin' Press.

Yalom, I.D. (2005). The theory and practice of group psychotherapy (5th Ed.). New York: Basic Books.